PRAISE FOR *OVERCOMING SERMON BLOCK*

Although written for the veteran preacher who is experiencing difficulty in the preparation and delivery of sermons, *Sermon Block* is a valuable tool for any preacher at any point in his/her ministry. In this concise volume, Tuck walks the reader through the essential steps of sermon development, from the initial call to preach through sermon delivery. Along the way, he offers both practical advice and personal anecdotes from a wide variety of academic homileticians and weekly practitioners. As a teaching tool for new preachers or as a good reminder for seasoned pastors, this volume is useful for both individual study and peer learning groups.

Tracy Hartman
Daniel O. Aleshire Professor of Homiletics and Practical Theology
Baptist Theological Seminary at Richmond, VA

A preacher might expect a book on overcoming sermon block to peddle a gimmick or a new magic pill. Instead, the noted William Powell Tuck advises the minister towards picking starting points, preparing, preaching, and evaluating, as part of a long arc of a preaching life. Preachers keep their wells fresh by keeping their calls in mind, taking the long look, respecting and engaging the text imaginatively, being clear, beginning and ending in ways that serve the sermon, using word pictures appropriately, and embodying the message with feeling consistent with a style that fits the preacher and serves communication.

The preacher who expects a quick fix will have to look elsewhere. The minister who is willing to cultivate a preaching life will find that like a well tended garden, such a life will bear fruit season after season. Along the way, Tuck points out that the preacher's own experience and the preacher's eye witness testimony are among the most engaging and truth-evoking aspects of preaching. One can say the same about this book: it has behind it the authority of Tuck's own life as preacher whose path to the sermon seldom, if ever, ended at a road block.

Ronald J. Allen
Professor of Preaching and Gospels and Letters
Christian Theological Seminary, Indianapolis

No one has ever cared more about good preaching than William Tuck, and *Overcoming Sermon Block* is the quintessential distillation of all he has thought and learned about the subject since he became a young minister years ago. Here he writes about everything from the calling and disposition of the preacher to the collection of material for preaching to the way sermons are imagined and produced. If I had had this book when I was a seminary student (also many years ago) I would have been a far better preacher than I was. I highly recommend it to others!

John Killinger
Former Professor of Preaching at Vanderbilt Divinity School and Princeton, pastor of 8 churches, and author of 70 books, including *The Changing Shape of Salvation* and *The Ministry Life: 101 Tips for New Ministers*

The act of preaching requires continual creativity, and preachers often find themselves in "dry times." The challenge of coming up with material that meets the needs of their congregations on a consistent basis is one that all preachers face. *Overcoming Sermon Block* addresses this challenge by dealing with every aspect of preaching, from invention to delivery, offering practical suggestions on how preachers can overcome those barren periods that make our preaching feel flat. It is, therefore, a must read for those who have just begun preaching, as well as a welcome refresher for those who consider themselves preaching veterans.

Doug Dortch
Pastor, Mountain Brook Baptist Church
Birmingham, AL

My first reaction on seeing this book was to question whether an author who has written or edited twenty books should be writing about sermon block, but William Powell Tuck brings a wealth of knowledge and experience to the task. Any preacher who has spent a Saturday afternoon fighting the temptation to go to desperatepreacher.com should read *Overcoming Sermon Block: The Pastor's Workshop*.

Brett Younger
Associate Professor of Preaching
McAfee School of Theology

Other Books by William Powell Tuck

The Way for All Seasons

Facing Grief and Death

The Struggle for Meaning (Editor)

*Knowing God: Religious Knowledge in the Theology of
John Baillie*

Our Baptist Tradition

Ministry: An Ecumenical Challenge (Editor)

Getting Past the Pain: Making Sense of Life's Darkness

A Glorious Vision

The Bible as Our Guide for Spiritual Growth (Editor)

*Authentic Evangelism: Sharing the Good News with Sense
and Sensitivity*

The Lord's Prayer Today

Through the Eyes of a Child

Christmas Is for the Young…Whatever Their Age

Love as a Way of Living

The Compelling Faces of Jesus

*The Left Behind Fantasy: The Theology Behind the Left
Behind Tales*

The Ten Commandments: Their Meaning Today

Facing Life's Ups and Downs

The Church in Today's World

The Church Under the Cross

Modern Shapers of Baptist Thought in America

The Journey to the Undiscovered Country: What's Beyond Death?

A Pastor Preaching: Toward a Theology of the Proclaimed Word

The Pulpit Ministry of the Pastors of River Road Church, Baptist (Editor)

The Last Words from the Cross

Lord, I Keep Getting a Busy Signal

OVERCOMING SERMON BLOCK

THE PREACHER'S WORKSHOP

WILLIAM POWELL TUCK

Energion Publications
Gonzalez, Florida
2014

Cover Photo by ID 25593013 © Aarrows | Dreamstime.com
Cover Design: Henry Neufeld

ISBN10: 1-938434-81-1
ISBN13: 978-1-938434-81-5
Library of Congress Control Number: 2014936500

Energion Publications
P. O. Box 841
Gonzalez, FL 32560

energionpubs.com
pubs@energion.com

For Emily
who has listened to my preaching
these many years
and has been my best critic,
my strongest supporter,
and consummate encourager

TABLE OF CONTENTS

SERIES PREFACE

Clergy, having left Seminary, quickly discover that there is much about congregational ministry that they never learned in school. They have touched upon it in a practical ministry class or a preaching class, and an internship may have allowed a person to get their feet wet, but as important as this foundational education is, there is much that must be learned on the job. It is not until one spends actual time in congregational ministry that one's strengths and weaknesses are revealed. Continuing education is therefore a must. Having collegial relationships is also a must. Who else but other clergy truly understand the demands of this vocation? In addition to ongoing continuing education and collegial relationships, it is helpful to have access to books and articles authored by experienced clergy.

This series of books, the second to be sponsored by the Academy of Parish Clergy, is designed to provide clergy with resources written by practitioners – that is by people who have significant experience with ministry in local congregations. The authors of these books may have spent time teaching at seminaries or as denominational officials, but they also know what it means to serve congregations.

The Academy of Parish Clergy, the sponsor of this book series, was founded in the late 1960s. It emerged at a time when clergy began to see themselves as professionals – on par with physicians and attorneys. As such, they not only welcomed the status that comes with professional identity, but they also embraced the concept of professional standards and training. Not only were clergy to obtain graduate degrees, but they were engage in ongoing continuing education. Following the lead of other professions, the founders of the

Academy of Parish Clergy saw this new organization as being the equivalent to the American Medical Association or the American Bar Association. By becoming a member of this organization one would have access to a set of standards, a means of accountability outside denominational auspices, and have access to continuing education opportunities. These ideals remain in place to this day. The Academy stands as a beacon to clergy looking for support and accountability in an age when even the religious vocation is no longer held in high esteem.

In 2012, the Academy launched its first book series in partnership with Energion Publications. This series, entitled *Conversations in Ministry*, fits closely with an important part of the mission of the Academy – encouraging clergy to gather in groups to support one another and hold each other accountable in their local ministry settings. The books in this first series are brief (under 100 pages), making them useful for igniting conversation.

This second series, *Guides to Practical Ministry*, features longer books. Like the first series, these books are written by clergy for clergy. They can be used by groups, but because they are lengthier in scope, they can go into greater depth than the books found the first series. Books in this series will cover issues like writing sermons, interim ministry, self-care, clergy ethics, administrative tasks, the use of social media, worship leadership.

On behalf of the Academy of Parish Clergy, the series' editorial team, and the publisher, I pray the books in this series will be a blessing to all who read them and to all who receive the ministry of these readers.

Robert D. Cornwall, APC
General Editor

ORIENTATION

Writer's block is a common complaint from many authors. They reach a point sometimes when they simply cannot produce anything worth reading. Preachers often encounter this same kind of roadblock when they attempt to prepare sermons. They stare at a blank page on the desk before them or a blank Microsoft Word page on their computer screen. Sunday is coming and they don't have a clue what to preach. They have experienced sermon block.

This book is offered as a possible solution to sermon block. Saturday night specials, last minute preparation, or spontaneous attempts at giving sermons will always leave the preacher frustrated, exhausted and dreading to preach. I believe that if a preacher carefully studies at a long range, prepares his or her sermons with a set yearly agenda, and follows a plan or Lectionary readings, he or she won't suffer from sermon block. The excitement and joy of preaching can be reborn or discovered for the first time by the preacher who gets in the preacher's workshop and crafts a stimulating message of the Christian Gospel — the good news of God's grace. How can this message be boring and humdrum? The preacher has an essential obligation not to be dull and lifeless in the pulpit. This requires careful preparation and long hours in the workshop.

The central focus of this book is two-fold: the minister's sermon preparation for delivering the sermon, and the actual act of delivering the sermon. I will examine the "nuts and bolts" of sermon preparation and the "pots and pans" essential for effective preaching. I will not concentrate primarily on the philosophy or theological dimensions of preaching. Instead, I will look at the necessary work of preparing, writing, and preaching a biblical sermon. Preaching can be exciting and challenging when the preacher is willing to invest the time and effort. I will lay out a blueprint to use in the preacher's workshop and then offer some further resources the preacher can use for assistance. Each chapter will conclude with questions and reflections. The following chapters are drawn from my years in teaching homiletics as Professor of Christian Preaching at the Southern Baptist Theological Seminary in Louisville, Kentucky, as an Adjunct Professor at the Baptist Theological Seminary in Richmond, Virginia, as a Visiting Professor at the University of North Carolina at Pembroke, and from my years in sermon preparation in my own workshop in the churches I have served as pastor. I want to thank my friend and fellow pastor, Rand Forder, for his careful proof-reading of the original manuscript. This book is a part of the series published by the Academy of Parish Clergy to encourage ministers to pursue excellence in ministry and in cooperation with Energion Publications.

Your Reason for Being in that High Place:

The Call to Ministry

When I was teaching preaching in the seminary, I required my students to write a brief paper about their call to ministry. I was amazed by the vast variety in the responses the students gave about their call. Several medical doctors, who were now seminary students, felt the call to go to selected mission fields as medical missionaries. Some of the students were right out of college, while others came from professions such as being attorneys, policemen, stock brokers, teachers, farmers and many others. They had come to seminary to prepare for ministry because they felt some kind of "nudge" from God to share the gospel with others. I believe a sense of call is essential if one is to preach the Word. From the earliest pages of the Bible we read about persons responding to God's call — Abraham, Moses, the prophets, including Jonah, Isaiah, Hosea, Micah and others, to Peter, James and John, leaving their fishing nets, and responding with the other disciples to the call from Jesus to follow him and become "fishers of men," Levi being called to leave his tax booth, to Saul's dramatic conversion and call on the Damascus Road. In a multiplicity of ways "the Word of the Lord came to them" and they heeded the call to witness for God.

The Variety of Calls to Ministry

Through the ages God has summoned men and women to proclaim the Word in a variety of ways. The call comes, nevertheless, with a "demand" to rely on the word of Jesus Christ for direction and assurance. "The concrete call of Jesus and simple obedience have their irrevocable meaning," Dietrich Bonhoeffer declares. "With it Jesus calls us in the concrete situation, in which he can be believed. He therefore calls concretely — because he knows that only in concrete obedience do we become free to believe."[1]

In the latter part of the nineteenth century, while a member at the Baptist Church in Whitewright, Texas, George W. Truett, who was considering becoming a lawyer, the congregation recognized his spiritual gifts and urged him to respond to God's call.[2] During a low time in his life, Frederick Buechner happened to drop into the Presbyterian church where George Buttrick was the preacher and had a dramatic conversion experience under Buttrick's preaching. Buttrick advised Buechner to enroll in Union Theological Seminary, which eventually led to his call into the ministry. He described this experience as the response to the "clack-clack of branches" from the "rattle" of the mystery of God's presence. In response to a woman who said to him one day, "I hear you are entering the ministry. Was it your own idea or were you poorly advised?" He said that she could not have heard the answer even if he had given it because:

> It was not an idea at all, neither my own nor anyone else's. It was a lump in the throat. It was an itching in the feet. It was a stirring in the blood at the sound of rain. It was a sickening of the heart at the sight of misery. It was a clamoring of ghosts. It was a name which, when I wrote it out in a dream, I knew was a name worth dying for even if I was not brave enough to do the dying myself and could not even name the name for sure.[3]

Sometimes one cannot easily describe the call one receives, but it is nevertheless definite. In his book, *Reflections on My Call to Preach*, Fred Craddock enumerates the influence on his spiritual journey of persons in Sunday school and worship in Central Avenue Christian Church in Humboldt, Tennessee and the Bethany Hills camp and conference and retreat center near Kingston, Tennessee. In response to the question of when he knew for sure that God had called him to preach, Craddock replied:

I didn't find it, or at least I didn't identify it. Not that I
think the certainty-producing moment is absolutely essential.
A call is of a piece with one's entire life of faith; it may be made
up of a constellation of small things: a stanza of a hymn, a
child's prayer, a friend's presence, a verse of Scripture, a greeting
card, an evening walk, or an encounter with a stranger. A recital
of modest events may not add up to a testimony satisfactory to
everyone, but I am sustained by it. In fact, I believe that one
could preach for a lifetime and yet not satisfy one or another's
desire for certainty.[4]

Some preachers can point to a definite occasion for their call.
Billy Graham, while a student at the Florida Bible Institute near
Tampa, Florida where he had preached in small churches, camp
meetings and in trailer parks for several months, finally fell to his
knees one night as he walked around a golf course and said he knew
he had been called to preach and responded with a yes. Although
there was no sign in the heavens or a voice from above, in his spirit
he knew he had been called to preach. Molly Marshall, who is now
president of Central Baptist Theological Seminary in Shawnee,
Kansas, said that her call to commit her life to a full-time Christian
vocation came when she was fourteen years old at a church camp
in Oklahoma.[5] Gardner Taylor, pastor for many years of the Con-
cord Baptist Church of Christ in New York (1948-1990), said that
while he was attending Leland College, his quick brush with death
when his car collided with another car, which lead to the death of
two people outside Baton Rouge, Louisiana, while he was spared
"turned me imperiously toward consideration of the meaning of my
life and the ultimate purpose of human existence."[6] He describes
this experience as both his conversion and call to ministry.

When he was nineteen years old, Henlee Barnette, later professor of Ethics at the Southern Baptist Theological Seminary in
Louisville, Kentucky for twenty-six years, was converted in a revival
meeting in his cotton mill town in North Carolina. After teaching
for some months in Sunday school and youth groups, his pastor
asked him if God was calling him to preach. He said that question

hit him like a thunderbolt, but he knew he had been wrestling with the matter and had to admit that he did feel a sense of call. He then returned to high school in the ninth grade after an absence of six years to complete his education and then to go on to Wake Forest College and later to Southern Seminary.[7]

Barbara Brown Taylor, the noted Episcopal preacher and teacher, traces the journey to her call from the time she went straight to Yale Divinity School from college, uncertain exactly why she choose to go to seminary. While at Yale she was confirmed at Christ Episcopal Church after a past "visitation" in a number of other denominations. After seminary, as she was working at Saint Luke's Episcopal Church in Atlanta, Georgia, she discovered that she was sensing a direction toward ministry. "I was so drawn to the work of ministry that I wanted to keep on doing it. I furthermore wanted to do it full-time, and in my mind there was only one way to do that," she confessed. "While I could not use the word *priest* in a sentence that began with *I*, that was what I wanted to be. In the language of the church, I was sensing a call."[8]

In my own spiritual pilgrimage, I became a Christian when I was a teenager at the age of sixteen, after I started working on the God and Country award in Scouting. I became active in Sunday school, worship, the youth choir, and all the other youth activities. The next year I was asked to be the youth week pastor, and I preached the sermon on Youth Sunday. My sermon title was "A Discovery of the Real Jesus," which reflected my personal struggle to know who this Christ really was. Soon I began to sense a "pull" toward ministry as my life's vocation. As I was walking to church one Sunday night in the early spring for the evening service, I remember pausing on the sidewalk under an apple tree, and surrendering to my call to ministry. Later I went to college to prepare myself for this goal.

A Sustaining Call

To me, a sense of call carries with it the strong affirmation that if I could do anything else, I should do that instead of ministry. But I have determined that a genuine call is so powerful that I would gladly pay to do the ministry I do — if I could afford it on my own. The inner satisfaction that comes from serving God in this way is so real that I cannot abandon it. I have also found that when ministry becomes difficult for whatever reason this commanding sense of call sustains me. I know I am not ministering to please or satisfy the wishes of others, as important as they may be, but my ultimate allegiance is to the Christ who has called me to follow him. His presence fortifies me during the dark and difficult days of ministering. Without that inner assurance, I believe many ministers are crushed under the pressures of trying to serve as a pastor and preacher. The load, endless demands, long hours, loneliness, continuous study, and lack of time with one's own family may lead to frustration, depression and even despair. A strong sense of call can be the central sustaining force in ministry that guides us to get the resources and assistance we need to do ministry effectively without burnout.

Called to Use Your Gifts

In Ephesians 4:11-16, the Apostle Paul speaks about the variety of gifts within ministry. Every pastor will bring a variety of gifts in ministry to the church he/she is called to serve. The minister will come to a church committing to that church the gift of ministry which he or she has. I believe that the highest gift that anyone can give to a congregation is his or her own individuality. The congregation should not expect her to be a "cookie-cutter copy" or "carbon copy" of some other preacher in the past or present, but will allow her to proclaim to the church the truth of God as she understands it through her own personality. I am convinced that on the day of judgment, as a pastor stands before God, God is not going to ask him or her, "Tony Smith or Sally Jones, why were you not like

Moses or Elijah or Paul or Dr. Barbara Brown Taylor or Dr. Fred Craddock in your ministry for me?" Instead I believe God will ask: "Did you use to the best of your ability the gifts which I gave you in ministry for me?" I hope that the minister will be able to say, "Yes, Lord, I gave you the best gifts I had to offer."

Some preachers make the mistake of trying to mimic the mannerism, gestures, voice, and style of some other minister that is totally unlike who they really are. We study and learn from other ministers, of course, but we should not mimic them. Strive to develop your own gifts to the best of your ability, practice and training. Paul Tournier has reminded us in his book, *The Meaning of Gifts* that "the supreme gift is the giving of oneself."[9] There is no greater gift we can offer to Christ than the commitment of whatever our special gifts are in service to him.

We should seek to develop our preaching gift so it will testify, honor, glorify and lead men and women to Christ and to deepen their commitment to follow him faithfully. I believe that God has called each of us to place our unique gifts on the altar of service for Christ. The gifts you have are different from mine and mine from yours, but my gifts are what I am challenged to use in my ministry to fulfill my special calling from God. Every minister wants to have an effective ministry. But we have to realize that our high calling is to be faithful to Christ in the use of our best gifts and not to be successful by the world's standards. Robert Cornwall reminds us in an excellent new book on spiritual gifts that "the gifts that we bring into our communities may or may not involve what we would deem natural talents, that is, innate abilities. The ultimate test of a gifts value is its usefulness in contributing to the welfare of the faith community and the world itself."[10]

Maintaining the Wonder of Your Call

To feel a sense of call by Christ can be an exhilarating experience that pulls us out of our routine and leads to living into a new and demanding adventure of faith. Unfortunately, after awhile, some ministers begin to lose the luster of that call. The minister needs to maintain his "childlike" wonder and retain throughout his life the freshness and vitality of the mystery of living. This childlike sense of wonder will lead us to continue to experience awe and wonder.

Worship is rooted in a sense of wonder and mystery. As we worship and proclaim the gospel message, we bow in awe before the God who created the universe and gave us life and called us to preach. We openly acknowledge that we cannot take God's presence for granted nor ever fully grasp the mystery of that holy presence which has summoned us into ministry. This mysterious presence demands that we always kneel in awe before the One who is holy and Wholly Other. Even as ministers we confess our sinfulness and the need for the redeeming grace of Christ.

Thumb through the Bible and the words "Behold," "Look!" "Attend!" "Listen!" summon us to experience admiration, wonder, surprise and joy as we worship and serve God. Worship in the Scriptures is often described as "the fear of the Lord." This "fear" arises out of a sense of awe, wonder and mystery. This sense of wonderment needs to continue to permeate our very beings and continuously enrich us. As long as we maintain that childlike sense of wonder, we will take delight in living, preaching and sharing the good news of the Gospel of Christ. Small children are open to wonder everywhere — in a bug on a bush, a bird in flight, a rock worn smooth by the flowing creek water, a piece of broken colored glass, a butterfly's wings, a wild flower, a rainbow, falling snow or rain. We need to continue to see life as Jesus has called us to see it through the eyes of a child. We have to remain childlike to be open to the mystery and wonder of life. To be childlike is to be continuously surprised, astonished, mystified, inspired, and amazed. As we look at the world around us and our ongoing responsibility to minister, we strive to the upmost of our ability to be open to the wonder of the world around us and the joy of ministering to God who loves us unconditionally. Loren Eiseley, the renowned anthropologist, has expressed picturesquely the wonderment of our world. "The world contains for all its seeming regularity, a series of surprises resembling those that in childhood terrorized us by erupting on springs from closed boxes."[11]

Remain open through prayer, meditation, study and abundant living to the mysteries all around us. Continue to be childlike. Open your ears, your eyes, keep an open mind, and stay alive to life. That does not mean that you will never have questions, doubts or fears. As human beings, even ministers, these challenges will be part of our spiritual journey. Others have known that difficult part of life's quest yet have still experienced the marvel of existence. "If there be a skeptical star I was born under it," W. MacNeile Dixon observed, "yet I have lived all my days in complete astonishment."[12] Of all people the minister has to retain the joy and good news of the Gospel message that she proclaims. We are charged "to declare good news" Paul reminds us in Romans 10:15 "How are they to proclaim him (Christ) unless they are sent? As it is written (quoting Isaiah 40:9) "How beautiful are the feet of those who bring good news!" Those who are "sent" are the called-out ministers who preach the good news of God's saving grace through Jesus Christ. It is not bad news or negative thoughts about life and living. David Bartlett writes that in his preaching classes he reminds his students that preaching is always good news.

Preaching is news; it is fresh, involving, surprising. It is not a repetition of tired formulas or one more self-serving plug for whatever program the deacons or the denomination have voted for that month. At the very least, therefore, I remind our students, preaching is a lively word. It is not a sin to be interesting.[13]

> Bartlett also acknowledges that since preaching is *good* news, he nags his new preachers not to nag. He challenges them to try an experiment in their preaching in which they avoid using even once phrases like "we ought," "you ought," or "we must" or "you must."[14] If the preacher can retain his vital sense of the good news of the Gospel, then he will not be using rhetorical ways of trying to scold or chastise his congregation but will seek to inspire and encourages them with the vibrant, surprising good news of God's grace.

In my opinion a call to ministry is vitally important to effective and vibrant preaching. This call will fortify and reassure the preacher during dry days which will come. Maintaining a readiness to be open to the surprising presence of God can keep the preacher tuned to the wonder and celebration of serving in the Kingdom's work. No agenda is more important for the preacher than her own spiritual nurture. The practice of the quiet life is essential to nurturing and strengthening one's own call. If the preacher is not growing in her own spiritual life she will not be able effectively to guide others in their spiritual quest. This thought will be expounded more in the next chapter.

Mark Hopper, Minister of Music and Organist at First Baptist Church, Henderson, North Carolina, wrote the following hymn, "Set Apart but Not Above," for his service of ordination to the ministry. The words challenge us to examine the real meaning of our call to serve God.

Set apart but not above,
    Leader servants heed God's call.
Each discerning, listening, learning,
    Each is shaped by gifts from all.
God handspun these gifts and talents:
    Prophecy, compassion, art,
Modeled love, impassioned teaching:
    Each one feeds the Kingdom's heart.

Not in front, but side by side,
    Called ones model Christ's command.
Synergy of love and service,
    Laboring, leading hand in hand.
Sometimes finding disagreement,
    Sometimes speaking truth in love.
Always one in God's great promise,
    Always listening to the Dove.

When ordaining God's new servants,

We can only gifts affirm.
God alone ordains, not people.
    God alone can call confirm.
Even then we each must listen,
    Old and wise or hungry youth,
Not to follow dogma blindly,
    But to struggle, seeking truth.

(Used by permission of Mark Hopper, 2013)

PERSONAL OR GROUP QUESTIONS & REFLECTIONS

1. Discuss whether you think a call is essential for a person to be a minister. If not, explain why you believe this.
2. If you have felt a call into ministry, share what that call was like and if you remember the time or place it occurred.
3. What do you think Levi and the other disciples like Peter, James and John had to change in their lives to follow Jesus? What would their families do for income when these men forsook their jobs and followed Jesus?
4. Read Fred Craddock's book, *Reflections on My Call to Preach*, and discuss his sense of call. Note how his call is similar to or different from your own call.
5. Reflect on how you think a preacher can keep his sense of wonder and the joy of the good news lively and paramount in his life and ministry.
6. In what sense are all Christians, lay persons as well as clergy, called to service for Christ?
7. What is your response to the hymn, "Set Apart but Not Above"?

The Importance of the Long Look:

Sermon Planning, Continuous Study, Bible Reading and Devotional Reflection

One of the main reasons why ministers become frustrated or fatigued in their preaching is that too often they wait until the last minute, Saturday night, to begin their sermon work for the next day. This sort of preaching has been characterized as "Saturday Night Specials." It is very difficult, if not impossible, to produce effective and meaningful sermons with such shallow preparation. Good preaching will arise from a preacher who spends careful hours in preparation during the week. I usually blocked off at least twenty hours a week for sermon preparation. Saturday night was given to finalizing or focusing the sermon. Before I got to this point I had done long range planning. Robert Reid and Lucy Hogan declare that they believe that the greatest challenge for preachers is "carving out time for sermon preparation and holding hard and fast to that commitment."[15]

Reasons for Long Range Planning

Whether the preacher looks at the year ahead and determines the texts on her own or follows the Lectionary for each Sunday, planning is essential. There are valid reasons for planning your yearly preaching schedule. (1) Planning will allow you to have variety in your sermon focus, while not preaching on the same theme every week. Some preachers seem to have only a one string guitar. No matter what the Scripture text, they always preach an evangelistic sermon. (2) Planning will help the preacher balance the use of the Old Testament and the New in choice of text, or if your tradition focuses on the Gospels and New Testament, this would help in your planning as well. (3) Planning will allow the preacher to vary the types of sermons preached – such as expository, narrative, topical, pastoral, doctrinal, and evangelistic sermons. (4) It will also help the preacher focus ahead on the holidays and holy days in the coming year, such as Mother's Day, Father's Day, Thanksgiving, the first Sunday in the New Year, as well as Easter, Christmas, World Communion. (5) Planning enables the preacher to get ahead of time the resources, commentaries, Bible studies, and other literature on the theme, for studying and preparation that will enrich the sermon. (6) Planning ahead allows the preacher to be on the lookout for illustrative material that might help clarify or make clear the central theme of the sermon. (7) Planning ahead will allow the Holy Spirit time to work in your thought and preparation over an extended period of time. It gives the preacher more time to engage in serious Bible study, exegesis and sermon crafting. (8) Planning allows the preacher to consider the particular needs of the congregation more thoughtfully. (9) Careful planning will reduce the anxiety and frustration that comes from last minute preparation. (10) Planning will assist all those who plan the worship service.

LONG RANGE PLANNING

Lectionary Preaching: If the preacher follows the Lectionary, then he will normally find the calendar divided into Advent, Christmastide, Epiphany, Lent, Holy Week, Eastertide and Pentecost over a three-year cycle of Scripture readings. Following the Lectionary offers the preacher a vast resource for worship planning. (1) The Lectionary will enable the preacher to deal with the whole gospel and not just parts of it. (2) It will assure the preacher of more careful focus on certain biblical passages that he might avoid otherwise. (3) It will make worship planning more effective because the Scriptures and themes are clearly in hand for the minister and the worship committee, if the church utilizes them. (4) It is also a good teaching tool because it focuses on the central doctrines of the Christian faith. (5) Following the Lectionary will also prevent the preacher from falling into the trap of using a civic or a denominational calendar as the basic worship guide. (6) With the focus on several Scripture passages each week, the preacher is reminded of the responsibility of declaring the biblical message and not merely parroting the major emphasis of secular society, one's denomination, or personal interests. (7) The use of the Lectionary permits the preacher to deal more thoroughly with the central themes of the faith. Many lectionary resources are found on the web and in books. On the web the preacher might consult *textweek.com*.[16] The most helpful book resource I have found is in the series edited by David L. Bartlett and Barbara Brown Taylor entitled *Feasting on the Word: Preaching the Common Lectionary* from Westminster John Knox.

Personal Planning: I have never felt that I was bound only to the Lectionary in my sermon planning. I have utilized it when I felt it was appropriate to the time and season, but at other times I have set my own plan for the year. (1) This plan has focused on the central themes of the Christian calendar like Advent and Easter. I cannot imagine preaching only one sermon in the Advent/Christmas season or Lenten/Easter season. I have usually planned a series of sermons for both of those seasons leading up to Christmas and Easter. (2) On other occasions I have planned a series of sermons on special needs I saw in my congregation. For example, when we had had a large number of deaths in our church family, I recognized a need to address the grief and bereavement of my congregation. I preached a series of sermons entitled "Facing Grief and Death" which was well received. On Wednesday nights we had talk-back sessions on the sermon themes. Through the years I have preached a number of series of sermon on the Lord's Prayer, the Beatitudes, the parables of Jesus, the miracles of Jesus, our Baptist tradition, etc. From time to time it would be good for all preachers to preach on the doctrines of their faith and their denominational heritage. (3) I have had special services focusing on communion and baptism. (4) The civic calendar affords the preacher an occasion to preach on the family on Mother's and Father's day. Memorial Day, Independence Day, Thanksgiving, Labor Day, New Year's Eve and other civic calendar events give opportunity to address other special themes from a biblical perspective. (5) Experimental sermons like monologues or dialogues can be planned for special Sundays like Youth Week, College Day, Children's Sunday or any time appropriate. (6) I have also planned series of sermons on theological, ethical and contemporary issues like pollution, the God is dead movement, situational ethics, creation, the nature of God, the *Left Behind* novels, the incarnation, death and the resurrection of Jesus and many others. (7) The preacher could do a series on major biblical themes like love, grace, hope, forgiveness, justice and mercy. (8) Sermons might address some of the perplexing questions that arise from people in your congregation like "Why do we die?" "Why did God let my child die from cancer?" "Where is God when the innocent suffer and die?" "How can we love our enemy?" "Why did Jesus have to die?" (9) The congregation can be asked to suggest to the pastor what Scripture passages or issues on which they would like him to preach. (10) The preacher can do a series on biblical characters like Abraham, Moses, David, the twelve disciples, or women of the Bible like Mary and Martha, Phoebe and Priscilla. The possibilities are only limited by the preacher's imagination. There are many older sources that I have found helpful like the ones by David Steel, *Preaching Through the Year,* J. Winston Pearce, *Planning Your Preaching,* and J. Ellsworth Kalas, *Preaching the Calendar,* published in 2004, and several web sites under "planning your preaching."[17]

CONTINUOUS STUDY

The long look will challenge the preacher to read widely throughout the year not just for sermon ideas, which will come, but for her own theological, biblical and spiritual growth. Include in this reading novels, theological and ethical books, and books on the Bible or current literature on contemporary issues, sermon books, and books on light and humorous themes. I also like to listen to books on tape, especially as I travel.

A sample of my recent reading list included novels like John Grisham's *Ford County, The Appeal*; Dean Koontz, *The Darkest Evening of the Year, Odd Apocalypse;* sermon books like *The Collected Sermons of William H. Willimon* and *The Collected Sermons of Fred B. Craddock* and sermons by Gardner C. Taylor; reflections on preaching *The Beauty of the Word: The Challenge and Wonder of Preaching* by James C. Howell; current issues like Ross Douthat's *Bad Religion*, Thomas L. Friedman and Michael Mandelbaum's *That Used to Be*, Eben Alexander, *Proof of Heaven*; theological works like Harvey Cox's *The Future of Faith*, N. T. Wright's *Surprised by Hope*, and *Love Wins* by Rob Bell; commentaries like *Luke* by Justo L. Gonzalez and *Lamentations and the Song of Songs* by Harvey Cox and Stephanie Paulsell; light reading like Jackson Brown's *Wit and Wisdom from the Peanut Butter Gang* and Bill Watterson's *The Essential Calvin and Hobbes.*

This type of reading not only keeps me abreast of the best in contemporary literature and the current social issues but exposes me to good writing and thinking. Sermon ideas, illustrations, stories and biblical insights leap out at me from almost every page. These readings expose me to thoughts and issues I am forced to engage whether I wanted to or not. They help in the planning of preaching by keeping me aware of the issues that society is confronting today and the challenges that are often being addressed to our religious beliefs from the scientific world and the intellectual community. Sermons often step out of the pages waiting to be confronted and written. These books are appealing to me or I simply enjoyed reading them. You will need to select those books that are most engaging for you.

SELECT A PARTICULAR BIBLE BOOK FOR STUDY

For awhile I have been studying the Gospel of Luke in a special way. That's the reason for the study of Justo Gonzalez's commentary on *Luke*. It is useful for the preacher to focus some special study during the year on a particular book of the Bible and study commentaries and books on that Bible book. This may not be your main sermon focus at the present time but this study will suggest sermon approaches later for you. Examine several commentaries at this time to get a wider perspective on your particular Bible book. This will certainly assist in preaching on it later. Be sure to make notes on themes, ideas, human needs and contemporary issues which might be addressed in your study.

SELECT A PREACHER FOR SPECIAL STUDY

I have personally found it helpful to study the life, style, methods and sermons of a particular preacher during the year. Over my lifetime I have examined dozens and have learned from all of them. These ministers can be contemporary, if there is sufficient material, or the person may be deceased but there is abundant, useful material, including a biography or autobiography and a number of sermon books. For example Barbara Brown Taylor has an autobiography and numerous sermon books one can study. The same is true for Gardner Taylor, Rick Warren and others. Past preachers that have been helpful to me are Harry Emerson Fosdick, Leslie Weatherhead, David H. C. Read, Leonard Griffith, Martin Luther King, Jr., Carlyle Marney and others.

I would encourage you to read their autobiographies or a biography on each one. This will introduce you to their background, education and pastoral experience. Some of them go into detail on how they prepared sermons. Read their sermons and notice their construction, introductions and conclusions, transitions, illustrations and use of the biblical text. Listen to their sermons on tape, if you can acquire any of them that way. This will let you hear their sermon and their style of delivery. Live with your preacher for some time, maybe a month or more. Read, analyze his sermons, learn his craftsmanship, notice the way he develops a text, the way the sermon flows and what grasps you as you read or listen to it. Don't try to mimic the preachers but learn from them. You will be amazed at how much this study will not only challenge you to do better preaching but will provide you some resources on how to do that.

BE PREPARED TO CAPTURE NEW IDEAS

Every preacher should carry a small notebook, lap top computer, or iPad to record new ideas when they come to you through your reading, conversation, lectures or sermons you hear, movies or TV shows you watch, travel or inspiration of the moment. How many of us have had a great idea for a sermon but failed to write it down and now it eludes us. It is amazing how quickly we can forget some idea or thought we heard or felt if we do not record it. Ideas may jump out at you at any time if you develop the homiletical eye. This small instrument, the notebook, will offer you countless reminders of things you read, saw or heard that can be used in your sermon making. It's a simple thing but amazingly important to good sermon preparation.

Develop a filing system, both in a cabinet and on your computer that works for you where you can keep sermon ideas, quotations, illustrations, biblical studies, preached sermons, etc. If you keep them on your computer, be sure and have them on some backup system like a flash drive or disk. You may want to file them under subjects, biblical texts, names or whatever works best for you. It can be as simple or as complex as you want, but some filing system is essential to do effective preaching. After I have preached a sermon, I always record where I preached it and the date and occasion, if it is unusual. I also record the resources that were helpful to me in the preparation of that sermon and where I got any quotes I used in the sermon.

THE PREACHER'S DEVOTIONAL LIFE

One of the most important disciplines a minister has to maintain is his spiritual or devotional life. If we are too busy for our own personal devotion, we are simply too busy. We have to keep our priorities right. Our personal spiritual nurture is absolutely essential. To fail here is not a minor shortcoming but neglect in a critical point of our own relationship to God. How can we guide others to worship and serve Christ if we neglect our own spiritual development? Our spiritual development affects our preaching as well. As we "labor" at our spiritual nurture, the amazing thing is that we are not only fed spiritually, but often sermon ideas arise out of our own devotional study and reflection. That is not our main purpose but it happens nevertheless.

To practice the disciplines of the spiritual life, the preacher needs to acquire the following: (1) Find a time of silence where you can seek to develop the "harvest of the quiet eye." Here you will try to shut out the noise of the world and "listen" for the "sound of the gentle stillness" of God's presence. Retire into yourself as into the soundlessness of God's Presence. (2) Select a particular place where you can be alone and will not be disturbed. Each minister has to decide that place for herself — your study at church, your home patio, den, or an isolated room in your house. (3) Set a definite time that you feel you can continue to honor for your devotion. Begin with a reasonable time period and let it progress as you honor this allotted time. If some interruption interferes with your schedule time, find some other moments in the day for your meditation. I will never forget the words of an Episcopal priest who was asked to meet with our group of ministers for a breakfast meeting. "I'm sorry," she responded, "but I can't come then. That's my quiet time." Ah, if we could be that dedicated and focused, our spiritual lives would be much more greatly enriched. (4) Relax by practicing breathing exercises. Take a few moments and inhale and exhale to relax your body. Open yourself quietly to God. (5) Your position in prayer is your own choice. It may be to kneel or you may sit at your desk or lie on your bed or walk. Choose the position with which you are comfortable. (6) Select a variety of resources for meditation. You will certainly select the Bible but use other devotional books that you find helpful from persons like Thomas a Kempis, Thomas Kelly, Richard Foster, Henri Nouwen, Kent Ira Groff, John Baillie, Joyce Rupp or Barbara Brown Taylor.[18] (7) Use your prayer time to adore God, offer your confession for your sins, affirm God's grace, offer thanksgiving for all your blessings and lift petitions for others. Meditate and reflect on God's call for you to serve at this time and in this particular place where you now are. (8) You may want to keep a prayer journal to record your prayers, thoughts or sermon ideas that come to you during this reflective time.[19] Let this be a time to feed your own personal spiritual need. This time apart in prayer will enrich your spiritual life and your preaching as well.

PERSONAL OR GROUP QUESTIONS & REFLECTIONS

1. What are some valid reasons for the preacher planning her sermons at least a year in advance? Or if you think this is not important, defend your reasons.

2. How can the Lectionary assist the preacher in sermon planning? Is the preacher obligated to follow the Lectionary in a rigid way?

3. Other than utilizing the Lectionary how might the preacher plan sermons ahead of time? What would be the strengths or weaknesses of not following the Lectionary?

4. Share some books with others in your group that you think you would like to read during this year and suggest how they might enrich your preaching.

5. Mention a particular preacher you admire and would like to study so you could learn how he or she prepares sermons.

6. Discuss how you try to keep ideas that come to you about sermons and how you save your sermons for future use. Do you believe that a sermon should be preached more than once? Is a sermon intended for one occasion only?

7.   Reflect on your own devotional life and consider whether it is well disciplined or only an occasional happening. What do you think this says about your own personal spiritual growth? Would assistance from a spiritual mentor be helpful?

OUR TEXT FOR THE DAY IS ...

FROM THE LECTIONARY, SERIES, OR SELECTED TEXTS

The biblical text is central for authentic preaching. A congregation does not gather on a Sunday morning merely to hear the opinion of the preacher. They come seeking a "Word from the Lord." This is a high expectation the congregation has of the one who claims she has had a "high calling." This expectation may be unrealistic for every gathering of the church and may leave the preacher grasping for heights he can rarely achieve. Nevertheless, if the preacher is not striving to discern a Word from the Lord, why does he dare stand in that elevated place?

Through meditation, prayer, study and reflection the preacher pours over a biblical text for the guidance of God's Spirit to "hear" the word to proclaim on Sunday. If the preacher is daring enough to say she is proclaiming a word from the Lord on Sunday, then she is obligated to allow the Spirit to guide her in her prayer, meditation and study of a particular biblical text. A lack of preparation and study, prayer and meditation because of laziness or busyness is not a badge the preacher wishes to exhibit. Preaching demands time, discipline, creativity, an inquiring mind, an open mind to the leadership of the Spirit, and a genuine awareness of the needs of the congregation he serves.

WHY USE A BIBLICAL TEXT

It should seem unnecessary to recommend that a preacher use a biblical text as the basis of a sermon. Yet many preachers have given sermons that have no biblical base at all. To me, there are a number of reasons why a preacher would lay a strong biblical foundation for her sermon. This does not mean that all sermons have to be expository, but I do believe all sermons should be biblically rooted.

Here are some reasons for this claim: (1) The Bible through the ages has been seen as the Church's chief authority. A sermon drawn from a biblical text, or a thematic sermon that is underwritten with a biblical text, will ring more authentically with the church's ancient tradition. (2) The use of a text may offer a greater sense of trust of the preacher because of the acceptance of the weight of the Bible as authoritative in the minds of the listeners. (3) A text will help the preacher resist delivering a sermon which is merely his own opinion. The preacher, of course, will give his interpretation of the text, but this should hopefully relate to the text being addressed. (4) The text ought to provide a "fence" which will determine the borders in which the preacher will frame the message. This may keep the preacher from going around the world in his sermon but focus instead on a prescribed area of thought. (5) The text may offer a realistic anchor for the listeners to secure the thrust of the sermon in their minds. In other words, a text may help make the sermon more memorable. (6) The text may allow the preacher to consider more difficult or controversial subjects than she could if approached on their own. The fact that the Bible discusses such themes may make the listener more tolerant toward these types of issues. (7) The text may serve as a bridge to meeting the human needs of the listeners and applying the meaning of the text to their lives.

CHOOSING A TEXT

If a preacher is to preach a biblical sermon, then the selection of a text is the first indispensable step. There are several possible ways in which a preacher might select a text, whether for Sunday morning or other occasions.. I will suggest five possibilities.

The Lectionary. Many denominational traditions are comfortable using the lectionary as their common source for sermon texts. Some lectionaries have generally provided three texts for a Sunday, while others have listed even more. Some provide Scripture readings not only for Sundays, the church's major holidays and festivals, but *The Revised Common Lectionary,* adopted in 1992, offers the preacher four choices of texts for a Sunday, one from a Psalm, an Old Testament selection, a Gospel lesson and an epistle reading. The Scripture readings are chosen by an ecumenical consultation of liturgical scholars and denominational representatives from the United States and Canada. The readings are presented in a three year cycle with each year focusing on one of the Synoptic Gospels. The wide assortment of biblical selections covers a large portion of the Bible but there are still numerous omissions.

The young minister, in particular, would be wise to utilize the lectionary especially in her early years in ministry. It provides a solid base for providing biblical readings for the pastor. The preacher will rarely be able to preach on all the texts but needs to select one for the central focus of the sermon. Choosing that particular text for preaching may require a hard decision and the elimination of others that are quite worthy. But trying to preach on all four of the texts in one sermon will likely be frustrating to the preacher and the congregation and lead the preacher down too many highways in one sermon. Be selective!

Lectio Continua. This term reflects an ancient practice of doing what is called "continuous reading" of the Bible where the preacher selects a portion of a Bible book and preaches on it, and then the next Sunday continues where he let off with another selection of the same book. And he continues until he completes the Bible book. If the preacher did this kind of preaching every week for many months, I believe the congregation would become very weary with this approach especially when the preacher reaches the "begets" passages. If a preacher wants to try this approach, she might begin with some shorter books like Ruth and Jonah in the Old Testament and James or the epistles of John or Philippians in the New Testament.

The preacher might focus on a selected Bible book for a month and then return to the lectionary or another approach instead of preaching for lengthy periods on this approach alone.

Subject or Thematic Selection. The preacher can also have a subject or theme on which she wishes to preach and then select an appropriate text that relates to the theme or subject. In one's study or awareness of a subject that will be helpful to the congregation or some person or persons in the congregation, the preacher may search for a text that will be suitable for that subject. If the subject is perverted prayer and proper prayer, for example, he may want to utilize a text like Matthew 6:5-7 where Jesus warns against the prayers of hypocrites and the contrast with secret prayer in your private room. If the subject focuses on the presence of God with us in difficult times, one might choose, for example, Romans 8:35-39 or John 14:27. In a Christmas sermon "Hospitality to the Highest," Harry Emerson Fosdick drew his text from Luke 2:6-7.[20] A sermon on anxiety might be based on the teaching of Jesus found in Matthew 6:34. Leonard Griffith, the former minister at the City Temple in London, England, has a sermon entitled "Risen But Not Recognized" referenced to Luke 24:13-31.[21] John Killinger connects with the story of the coming of the Wise Men (Matthew 2:1-12) in a Christmas sermon entitled "A Gift that Matters."[22] All of these sermons offer thematic sermons that had a text but were not textual or expository sermons. The idea of the sermon likely came first and the text later.

The preacher has to be careful in this approach that she does not go "chasing rabbits" that are of interest only to the preacher and not the congregation. Rather than trying to select such a subject text on a weekly basis the minister needs to plan his preaching some time in advance in a carefully organized effort. This will allow the necessary time to approach Scripture texts that are appropriate for the subjects. A sermon series on the basic beliefs of one's own denomination can be useful in this kind of preaching. A Scripture text that captures the thrust of each of the doctrines set forth can be selected. A subject series of sermons on the doctrines of the faith like sin, salvation, grace, love, redemption, resurrection, can easily find appropriate texts for such themes. A sermon series on contemporary social and ethical issues like racism, poverty, war, peacemaking, justice, pollution, etc. can easily find Scripture texts that are adequate for these subjects. This approach will challenge the preacher to match authentically the text with the subject at hand and not twist it in a way that is inappropriate for the text.

Self-Selection of a Text. This approach is similar to the thematic approach in that the preacher selects a Scripture himself for the sermon. The difference is that the preacher may not have a subject in mind but personally chooses at text or biblical passage on which to preach. The sermon may be expository, textual or thematic based on the passage selected. An expository sermon will treat a larger portion of Scripture while the textual approach may utilize only a verse of Scripture. The twenty-third Psalm, for example can be preached as an expository sermon focusing on each verse in the psalm or be thematic as one addresses the major themes in the psalm or textual, if one chooses to select only one of the verses for his text like "The Lord is my shepherd" or "he restores my soul." If one selected the one verse, Romans 1:16, for example; it could be preached thematically under subjects like: (I) Unashamed Christians. (2) The Meaning of the Gospel. (3) The Power of God. (4) For Salvation. (5) To Everyone who Believes. That could be called a textual sermon or expository.

Again this approach requires the preacher, if he is to avoid "fishing" for sermons at the last minute by roaming through the Bible, to plan ahead in selecting the texts he wants to use in his preaching over the next three, six or twelve months. The texts that are the best for the life of the church at this given time may arise out of knowing the theological needs of the congregation, question-naires the congregation have completed, comments he has heard raised about the Bible, or his own private devotional study. This is not a method to preacher should use all the time. This "hunt and peck" approach can get frustrating and lead to a limited and parochial sermon agenda.

Human Needs. Sermon texts may also be selected that address human needs of members in one's congregation. Our parishioners struggle with personal problems of all kinds, loneliness, depression, anger, fears, pessimism, failure, suicide, aging, illness, suffering, death and many others. An acknowledgement of these struggles can be essential to identifying with one's congregation, and from this awareness, some of the preacher's most helpful preaching will address these needs. Textual sermons or thematic sermons may also speak to these issues. No preacher can ever speak to all the needs of her congregation, but sermons that are aimed in that direction are usually well received. The preacher can plan a series of sermons to try to relate to these needs. I have preached several series aimed at this type of preaching: "Making Sense of Life's Darkness" and "Facing Life's Ups and Downs."[23] This approach is similar to selecting a text for a subject so the preacher has to be careful to plan ahead and make certain that the Scripture passage is appropriate for the sermon. Expository sermons can also address human needs if the application of the text is authentically related to a genuine need. Again the preacher should refrain from making this her only kind of preaching.

How to Study a Text for Preaching

Once the preacher has selected her text for the sermon then begins the important task of determining the real meaning of the text. Authentic preaching will flow only from preachers who are willing genuinely to engage the Scripture passage and determine the proper interpretation of the text. "To preach biblically," Leander Keck reminds us, "is to take full account of the concrete issues to which the text was addressed in the first place."[24] According to Keck, this challenges the preacher to determine what the biblical writer found necessary to say not by focusing on "truth in general but by needs in particular."[25] This forces the preacher to probe deeply into the text to be certain of its proper significance. No quick or superficial glance at the text can achieve this purpose. The preacher needs to be willing to invest the necessary hours in sermon preparation in her study to achieve this purpose. The following suggestions are offered to help guide the preacher in this endeavor.

Personal Reflection. Begin by reading the text without any use of commentaries or other helps and see what you believe it is saying. If you can read Greek or Hebrew, then read the text in the original languages or use a Hebrew or Greek Interlinear version which gives you a literal English translation of the text. Use various translations to get a clearer grasp of the text. I have found the following translations helpful: *The New Revised Standard Version, The New International Version, The Revised New English Bible, Good News for Modern Man, The James Moffatt Translation of the Bible,* and *The New Testament in Modern English by J. B. Phillips.* Some older translations like *The King James Version* bear some words whose meaning have completely changed like "prevent" which really means "to go before." Spend some time comparing translations until you feel like you understand the sense of the biblical passage. Jot down the thoughts that come to you on your first reading of the text. Reflect on the text slowly and mull it over in your thinking until you feel you have gotten inside it. Later you can compare these original thoughts with your insights after you do further study with commentaries.

Mine the Text. Next use your study time to dig deeply into the meaning of the text. This exegesis will require probing into the Greek or Hebrew of the text if you can read the biblical languages. Do not hesitate to dig deeply into the text to determine its true status. Ask serious questions and probe the best insights of biblical scholars as you study through various commentaries and other books. Search the multi-volume sets like Gerhard Kittel and Gerhard Friedrich's *Theological Dictionary of the New Testament* and G. Johannes Botterweck's *Theological Dictionary of the Old Testament.* Use word studies of the New Testament like the ones by A. T. Robertson or Marvin Vincent to examine the meaning of selected words in the text. Ask questions of the text like the following: (1) When was this biblical passage written and where? (2) Who wrote it? (3) What type of literature is it — poetry, drama, history, a letter, a parable, an allegory, etc.? (4) What seems to be the main intention of the passage? (5) What is its theological message? (6) What is the historical context of this text? (7) What is its context in the book of the Bible where it is located? (8) What is its connection with the passages before it and that follows it? (9) Is it a genuine Scripture passage or a spurious text the writer might be quoting or an interjection into the passage? Reading commentaries and using scholarly word studies can help determine this.

These are just a few of many questions you can use to investigate or mine the text. In my book, *A Pastor Preaching: Toward a Theology of the Proclaimed Word*, I suggest a dozen or more you can use.[26] Other professors of preaching like James Cox, Fred Craddock, Tom Long and others offer similar questions the preacher can use to address the text.[27] Craddock suggest that the preacher should also ask "what is the text doing?" The preacher, he suggests, needs to be aware not only of what is being said in the sermon he will preach but what is being done in the sermon. This means that just as the sermon is informed by what the text is saying, the function of the sermon is informed by what the text is doing. This awareness, he suggest, arises from the historical context of the text. If the text is celebrating, encouraging, confessing, punishing, informing, correcting, persuading, etc., this will inform you what it is trying to do. If the preacher wants the sermon to do what the text is doing, then the preacher should hold on to the function of the sermon in the design of her own sermon as well as in the interpretation.[28]

Implement the Text. Having probed deeply into the text and determined what it is saying and doing, now the preacher has to bring the text into the thought and life of the listener. Explaining, interpreting, displaying or translating the text has to lead to a claim on the listeners. This is the time Cox suggests that the preacher has to make the text real and true in the life of the hearers.[29] The Gospel has to become incarnate in their lives. "Something happens between text and people: a claim is made, a voice is heard, a textual will is exerted," Thomas Long declares, "and the sermon will be a witness to this event."[30] This can happen best in the preaching context where the pastor is preaching to the congregation she knows from having ministered pastorally to them. When the pastor knows the congregations' needs and the congregation knows the preaching pastor, and a pastoral relationship has been established, communication and execution of the sermon are more likely to transpire.

James Howell calls the text "a window into the broader reality of our faith."[31] The text may indeed be a window, but might it not also more importantly be a "mirror" into our lives where we are confronted with an image of our real selves. The text as a mirror might be where we see what we are challenged to be, to become, witness to, how we are to serve, love, show mercy, find forgiveness, experience grace, salvation and discipleship and more. The ultimate goal in using a text is not primarily imparting information, although that may happen, but in changing lives. A sermon that allows the listeners to think, feel, and respond to the text in a personal way and not in a prescribed fashion allows the Spirit to work through the text in His own surprising and engaging manner in and through the preacher and the listener.

Selecting, investigating, implementing and preaching a text can be a demanding and time consuming process, but it offers the preacher, who will take the time, rewards and satisfaction that the preacher and congregation can cherish. If the Bible is our chief authority and the basis of our preaching, how can we not give it our preeminent time and efforts?

PERSONAL OR GROUP REFLECTIONS & QUESTIONS

1. How do you determine what text you will preach on Sunday?
2. If you have selected a subject to preach on, how do you arrive at an appropriate passage of Scripture or a particular verse for that theme?
3. Have you found the lectionary helpful? If so, in what way. If not, what have you found to be its limitations?

4. In what ways have you tried to determine the meaning and application of the text?

5. Select a biblical passage like Matthew 14:23-33, "Jesus walking on the water," and discuss how you would investigate this text and show its relevance, if any, for your congregation.

6. Discuss in your group or reflect yourself on what Bible translations you have found most helpful and explain why.

7. Tell how you move a text from the biblical passage into the thought and life of your listener.

8. If you have preached any series of sermons, share some titles of your series. How did your congregation respond to the various series?

WHAT'S THE PREACHER SAYING ANYWAY?

THE CENTRAL FOCUS OF THE SERMON

An elderly experienced pastor was asked one day by a young minister just beginning her preaching preparation: "How many points should a sermon have?" Pausing for a moment, the older minister responded: "At least one." Oh, I know some homileticians don't like to talk about sermons having points any more. The old joke was that a sermon had to have three points and a poem.

Following Fred Craddock's inductive approach to sermonizing, the emphasis of many teachers of homiletics today is not so much on trying to make points in a sermon but to follow the intent of the text. We will reflect more on this discussion later, but I want to argue strongly that every sermon has to have some central focus. I have heard too many lay persons and fellow ministers complain after listening to a sermon: "What in the world was that preacher trying to say?" Or "I couldn't make any sense out of what she was saying." Or "Do you know what that gibberish was all about?"

I will never forget going to a preaching conference on narrative preaching several years ago and hearing a young man come before our group of preaching professors and preach, no, tell a brief story and then walk off the podium. No Scripture was read. There was only the story. Several of us looked at each other and asked: "What was the point of the story?" And further, in what way was it really a sermon, and if so, what did he say? The point on which I am insisting here is that every sermon to be understood by the listeners has to have a focus point — first in the mind of the preacher, if it is to be communicated to the listeners. This is true whether the sermon is narrative, textual, expository, theme centered or whatever approach is used. If the preacher does not know what he "is driving at," then how can the congregation possibly "catch it?"

THE CENTRAL FOCUS OF A SERMON

Every sermon has to have at least one central idea or focus. The preacher will determine this from her careful investigation of the text as I suggested in the last chapter or from the analysis of the study of the subject to be preached. This central focus is the theme, key idea, "the what" of the sermon's meaning. "I have a conviction that no sermon is ready for preaching, not ready for writing out," John Henry Jowett declares, "until we can express its theme in a short, pregnant sentence as clear as a crystal." Musing further, he observes, "I find the getting of that sentence is the hardest, the most exacting, and the most fruitful labour in my study."[32]

This may be the most difficult and time consuming task the preacher has to come to grips with in the early stages of the sermon preparation. Hopefully and normally, it will arise through your study of the text or from the reading you are doing on the sermon topic you have chosen to pursue. Shaping this central focus can help you frame and craft the sermon as it flows from your under-standing of the direction in which the sermon is moving. Often this direction arises from the intention of the biblical text as you grasp it or from the development of the theme of the sermon which may arise from a specific occasion, special need or an indomitable sense of direction from your study.

In the past, homileticians would use the phrase "central idea," "proposition," "subject," or "theme" to convey what the intent of the sermon was. The argument to move away from this was based on the view that a sermon was not an essay where the preacher was presenting points that came out of this one central idea of the text. It was also suggested that once the preacher discovered the "central idea" in the text, it was utilized to direct the sermon and then the text was abandoned. Fred Craddock, Thomas Long and others have argued further that the biblical text is not basically propositional in its context and should not be used to make the sermon a list of propositions to which one has to assent or agree. Rather than deducting a central point from a text, this approach calls for an inductive approach in which the preacher invites the listener to make his or her own discoveries in the process as the sermon is delivered.[33]

While I agree with much in this preaching method, I maintain, nevertheless, that in either deductive or in inductive preaching the central focus of the sermon is essential. This central focus does not have to be spelled out into propositions but may instead unfold or flow like a stream or reach out like branches, etc. On the other hand, I heard an interim pastor over a period of months move his sermon forward by saying "point number one" and "point number two," etc. And it was still a powerful message each week that kept the attention of the congregation, because his focus was clear and his striking language and use of the text were powerful. This sermon approach will not work for many, and I do not feel it is very effective generally today. To assume that the central focus must first arise or only can come from the text is unrealistic. However, if the preacher follows the lectionary rigidly, then the focus has to come first from the text.

Sometimes the sermon has to focus on special occasions like the Church Founder's Day, Anniversary Sunday, Senior Adult Sunday, Stewardship Emphasis, Youth or Children's Sunday. Simply to use the lectionary text on these occasions, in my opinion, would be inappropriate. The preacher begins with the theme for the occasion and then uses the theme of a proper text to guide the sermon. I do not feel that it is wrong to begin a sermon sometimes from a subject, special need or emphasis, doctrine or some other theme and then select a text to communicate that emphasis. Why miss the opportunity to speak to a special requested theme for a church and use instead a lectionary text that may have nothing to do with the occasion? A sermon series may arise out of texts like "The Last Words of Jesus from the Cross" or "The Lord's Prayer." Other series like "The Common Struggles of Life" or "Learning How to Pray" may rarely begin with texts.

WHERE DO SERMON IDEAS COME FROM?

The answer is quite literally everywhere. I have found sermon ideas, suggestions, thoughts or themes arising from (1) reading the lectionary texts, (2) reading the Bible, (3) my personal devotional time, (4) studying the Bible, theological and other religious books, (5) reading sermons of noted preachers, (6) reading novels, plays or short stories, (7) reading the daily newspaper or magazines like *Time* or *Newsweek*, (8) watching TV, going to the movies or a play, (9) conversations with people, (10) pastoral ministry within my parish, (11) questions that are raised to me by members of my congregation, (12) letters, email or the internet. This is the serendipity factor in preaching where one finds valuable or delightful things when one is not seeking them.

If we have developed the "homiletical eye," we will learn to see and hear ideas that become sermon starters for us. Frederick W. Robertson, the late Brighton, England minister, used to say that he could not "light his own fire." Many sparks leap at us along life's way, and the discerning mind will feel the warmth of the flame that is lit. Many will help light our sermonic fires through our years of ministry.

Some time ago one of our church members told me that he never seemed to get an answer to his prayers. "I wonder," he complained "if God ever listens or really hears our prayers?" This ignited in my mind a sermon which I later entitled "Lord, I Keep Getting a Busy Signal." My Scripture text was Romans 8:26-27. My central focus was stated: "Although it may seem at times as though God does not listen or respond to our prayers, be assured that God indeed hears us and responds in God's own way not always with an answer but with a presence." In my reading some theological books on the cross, I became aware that the church often fails to understand its authentic mission to center its ministry on the cross of Christ. I prepared a sermon under the title "The Church under the Cross" with my Scripture text as 2 Corinthians 8:17-21. The central focus was "having been reconciled to God by the sacrificial death of Christ on the cross, the church is challenged to share this message of love with others and to live the Christ-like, cross-like way of life." This central focus may be a simple statement or a complicated one, but it will help drive the whole movement of the sermon.

WHAT'S THE POINT OF THE SERMON?

A central focus of a sermon will help you determine what you hope to accomplish with the sermon. This might be called the "why" of the sermon. The purpose should act like a magnet and pull the sermon forward to accomplish its aim or intention in the listeners' response. It should reveal what the sermon is all about — you are preaching 'in order that …" It should act like a "lodestar" that streaks through the sermon and serves as a guide throughout the whole sermon. The central focus might ring out in the sermon like the words of Martin Luther King Jr. in his famous sermon "I Have a Dream" delivered in Washington, D. C. "I have a dream" echoes again and again throughout the sermon as depictions of this dream are enumerated. There are many forms the central focus can take. A few of the many possibilities might include the following:

The Intention of the Text. Having determined the basic intention of the text from your investigative study, you would seek to follow that known intention as your central focus. This might be what follows most of your studies for lectionary preaching. For example, a sermon on the text about the Prodigal Son might have as its central focus the words from Henri Nouwen: "Though I am both the younger son and the elder son, I am not to remain them, but to become the Father."[34] This sermon would show how both sons are prodigal in different ways, one in a trip away from home and the other a self-righteous sinner at home. But the central focus would lead to the declaration about the radical grace and love of

the Father. In the Scriptures where Jesus tells his disciples that he
is giving them a new commandment, found in John 13:34-35 and
15:9-17, I believe that one could draw from the intention of this
text the following central focus: "Jesus' love for us is our guide and
example and the measurement for whether or not we have loved
properly." The beatitude, Blessed are the poor in spirit" (Matthew
5:3) might have as its central focus drawn for the intention of that
text, "Happy are those who have emptied themselves of vain pride
in the awareness of their own inadequacy and sin and have humbly
accepted the rule and power of God in their own lives." Following
the intention of the text, the central focus would carry forward this
intention in its spelling forth the meaning of the text.

The Teaching Approach. Another possible objective for the sermon may be a teaching approach. The pastor in every congregation
is the chief biblical and theological teacher. The pulpit provides a
legitimate place to teach one's congregation. A sermon series offers
the preacher a means of teaching various doctrines or other spiritual
matters in more depth than is possible in a single sermon.

A series on the Apostle's Creed, your denomination beliefs, the
Beatitudes, the Lord's Prayer, Jesus' teaching on love, the psalms, or
the difficult sayings of Jesus, can have as its main focus teaching the
congregation so it can grow in the knowledge of the Christian faith.
Many people in our congregations are uninformed about many of
the basic beliefs of the Christian faith and teachings found in the
Bible. Teaching is an essential part of the pulpit ministry.. Your ultimate goal may be more than just teaching or sharing information.

To Change the Attitude or Life Style of Your Listeners Another purpose of the sermon could be changing the mind, attitude,
philosophy, perspective, or way of living of the listeners in your
congregation. You are preaching so that prejudices may be altered,
new insights unveiled, selfishness changed to service of others,
doubt to faith, shallow thinking into more mature thinking, dis-
torted Christian perspectives into sound beliefs, or unbelief into
belief. A sermon I preached on "A Theology of Ecology," based in
Genesis 1:26-31, not only informed my congregation about the

immensity of the problem of pollution, but I also spoke of our responsibility as Christians to be "caretakers" of the earth God has created. Many in the churches have not acknowledged that we along with others are responsible for the problems of pollution in our world, and as Christians we have to develop a theology that helps us turn from being those who are helping to destroy our planet and become those who are striving to save it.

A sermon on the beatitude "Blessed are the peacemakers," (Matthew 5:9), might seek to move the listeners from merely talking, thinking, or discussing peace to actually becoming peacemakers. The sermon could be called "Wage Peace."

I preached a sermon, "What Color Is Love?" based on Genesis 1:27 and Galatians 3:26-29 that dealt with the evil and deep roots of racial prejudice and challenged the church to help build bridges in human relationships and remove all barriers through the love which we have seen in Christ. A sermon could be preached on "The Challenge of Religious Freedom" with Scripture texts Leviticus 26:12-13 and John 8:31-36 and focus on the necessity of not merely accepting the fact that we have religious freedom in our country but to help the congregation to realize that religious freedom is always under challenge and the church has to remain diligent to assure it will not be lost to forces that seek to undermine it.

A Call to Faith or to a Deeper Commitment to Christ. The purpose of the sermon could involve leading someone to making an initial commitment of trust in Christ as Lord and Savior. The text might be drawn from the story of the conversation of Jesus and Nicodemus about the necessity of the "new birth" (John 3:1-10) or from the parable of the Lost Sheep in Matthew 18:10-14. Some preachers try to turn every sermon into an evangelistic sermon, but I believe that often can be a violation of the meaning of the text. The listener may "overhear" the good news of the gospel and still respond but the preacher needs to honor the genuine meaning of the text.

The sermon could be geared toward leading Christian listeners to a deeper commitment to following Christ as Lord. A sermon

could be drawn from the text Matthew 5:13 where Jesus said to his
disciples, "You are the salt of the earth." This text reminds us of the
penetrating, impacting, preserving, joyful and purifying force of the
Christians in the world and the challenge for us to indeed be that
factor in the world. Another sermon might be based on Ephesians
4:11-16 where each Christian is summoned to use his or her gifts
in ministry for building up the church to do the ministry Christ
has called us to accomplish.

A Commitment to Service. The sermon might be a summons
to serve Christ more effectively in one's community or around the
world. Such a sermon could focus on Jesus' parable found in Luke
17:7-10 or Mark 10:44, where Jesus says that the greatest of all
is the servant of all. The focus is on the Christian whose servant
ministry calls us not to see what we can get out of the world but
what we can do in service for Christ who lived and modeled this
servant ministry for us in the "towel and basin" service at the Last
Supper and in his death on the cross.

A Summons to Arrive at Your Own Conclusion. The sermon may
be drawn from a passage of Scripture where the preacher offers no
clear purpose but invites the listener to arrive at her own conclusion
as she follows the movement of the sermon and is then given the
opportunity of taking a path that addresses her particular need or
hope. A passage like Mark 1:16-20, where Jesus calls his disciples
might be such a text. What has Jesus called you to do? What "nets"
will you leave?

These are a few samples but you can make your own list and
add many others. Strive to make your sermon focus clear and let
it carry your sermon forward toward what conclusion would be
appropriate.

COMMUNICATE AND TRANSLATE YOUR TEXT FOR YOUR LISTENERS

The preacher has to communicate his message to the congregation in a language, tone, style and approach that will make them

want to listen. One of the chief complaints from congregations is that the pastor too often speaks in a language that is too technical, abstract, or theologically obscure. Some preachers feel like they have to share the pots and pans they used to "cook" the sermon, that is, while they were doing their investigation and preparing it. The listeners don't want to hear about all the sources, quotes, or Hebrew or Greek word studies you were involved in.

Put the sermon in a language they can follow as you strive hard to "translate" the message so the listeners can grasp its central focus. Clarity is the answer not obscurity. This can be achieved not only through understandable language but also through stories, word pictures, narrative, humor, and by inviting the listener to participate in the sermon. With the central focus clearly in hand, the preacher is charged with communicating that message in the best way she can.

PERSONAL OR GROUP REFLECTIONS & QUESTIONS

1. Where have most of your sermon ideas come from? Were they first sensed from Bible study or in some other way?
2. Select one of the biblical texts mentioned above like 2 Corinthians 8:17-21 or another one and discuss what you think is the central focus of that text. Put that central focus in a clear sentence.
3. What do you think are some legitimate purposes for having a central focus for the sermon? Which one would you find most helpful and which one do you utilize most often?
4. Name some preachers you believe have a clear focus in their preaching and what means they implore to achieve this goal?
5. How do you avoid displaying your diligent sermon investigation and preparation (your pots and pans) in your sermon when you deliver it?
6. Do you think the criticism is valid that preachers often preach in theological jargon the listeners do not understand? If so, what can the preacher do to overcome this weakness?

BEGINNING AND ENDING THE SERMON:

INTRODUCTIONS AND CONCLUSIONS

Many of us can remember sitting in church, a denominational meeting or a special conference and hearing someone like Fred Craddock begin his sermon in such a griping way that we simply had to listen. We all know when the sermon has been introduced well. The way a preacher begins her sermon will likely determine whether the listener will stay with the preacher for the rest of the sermon. Unfortunately studies have revealed that introductions are consistently the weakest part of a sermon. An otherwise good sermon can be ruined if the introduction is not carefully planned.

SOME PRINCIPLES FOR GOOD INTRODUCTIONS

Obstacles to Overcome. The preacher needs to be aware that even in the best prepared worship services, when he stands up to speak he will be met by a congregation that is often tired, sleepy, or distracted by thoughts about lunch, problems at home or work, projects that are being resolved in the listeners' mind and a dozen other personal reflections. Somehow the sermon introduction has to penetrate that distraction and call the listener to be attentive to the message. This awareness should come as a challenge to every preacher.

Get Attention and Create Interest. The preacher is not likely to get the attention of the congregation by saying, "The text for this morning is…" That will likely only create a yawn since it has already been announced in the Sunday's order of worship. The attention and effort to create interest will come if the preacher, for example, uses a striking sentence or quote, a startling statement, a witty, humorous or amusing incident, a vivid word picture, a personal experience, a vivid illustration, etc. The introduction is saying to the congregation, "Here is why you should listen to this sermon."

I began a sermon on prayer once with this comment: "Prayer is really kids' stuff, you know." I paused for a moment and then added, "the man said to me." That startling statement did indeed get their attention. I then invited the listeners to go with me on an inquiry to see if prayer was really meaningful for adults as well as children.

Move Rapidly into the Sermon. Some preachers linger too long in the introduction and do not move forward into the main movement of the sermon. They keep repeating the obvious and seem to be jogging in place unable to advance. I heard it said of one preacher that he took so long to dress his sermons that they caught cold. Do not loiter in the lobby, but let the introduction propel you forward. Let the introduction introduce and move on.

Use Brevity in the Introduction. The introduction is not the place to explain all you plan to say in the entire sermon. John Killinger says the introduction is like a master of ceremonies. "They set up the audience for the next guest, then quickly bow out of the way."[35] How brief? Aim for a paragraph or two, half a page, or no more than one-hundred words. Remember you have the rest of the sermon to disclose your central focus.

Appropriateness. Let the introduction be appropriate for the central focus or theme of your sermon, the occasion or special event, if that is true. If your sermon is not based on the lectionary and is instead on a special church anniversary service, use an introduction which fits that particular sermon. The introduction should reveal that you are indeed going to celebrate the 150th anniversary of their church and call them to continue to link their church with Jesus who has called the church to be a servant people. This type of introduction would note both the celebration of the church's history but the challenge that lies before the church in the present and future. The same introduction is obviously not appropriate for every sermon, yet many preachers rarely change the way they introduce their sermons.

Concreteness. Sometimes preachers have a tendency to exaggerate numbers or to speak in generalities rather than to speak realistically. The preacher may refer to thousands of people being killed in a military battle or describe a problem in such vague sweeping statements that the listeners can't really get their minds around it. A plane crashed in Atlanta, Georgia several years ago and forty-one people were killed. A preacher I know introduced his sermon on "The Will of God" with the news item from the morning newspaper and asked the question which was on the lips of many, "Why did God let that happen?" It was a concrete focus that was on the minds of his congregation that Sunday.

Conductive. A good introduction, according to John Killinger, should be conductive and lead the listeners into the sermon.[36] That is, the introduction should not simply give a grand image or thought that creates such a magnificent attention-getting experience and then leave the congregation wondering what it really has to do with the rest of the sermon. If there is no substance that comes subsequently, the congregation will not continue to listen. "The introduction should be anticipatory," James Cox declares, "that is, it should successfully point to the main discussion. It must decrease while the body of the sermon increases."[37] But if the introduction is an exaggerated "shout" or simply a cry for attention and no sermonic meat follows on the table which is spread, the congregation will leave the spiritual table hungry and unfed.

The introduction should generate anticipation that is later realized in the body of the rest of the sermon. Thomas Long puts it this way: "A sermon introduction should anticipate the whole sermon, but it should also connect directly to the next step of the sermon."[38] When introducing the sermon, the preacher not only gets attention but invites the listeners to move forward with her in the journey which lies before them moving one step at the time.

A Promise to Keep. Thomas Long also suggests that an introduction should make a promise to the listeners which they likely want kept.[39] If the introduction is offering a promise of what is to follow, the preacher had better deliver. Long argues whether this places the minister in a bind to deliver what the congregation wants to hear or can he not address the demands of the gospel as well as the comforts of God. I do not believe that genuine preaching can avoid the heavy demands of the Gospel without offering what Dietrich Bonhoeffer calls "cheap grace." Every sermon introduction may not offer such a promise as the congregation may wish, but surely every sermon should offer the promise that the question, issue, hope, fear, etc. alluded to in the introduction will be addressed in the rest of the sermon to follow.

Present the Human Need. The introduction may also present the human need the sermon will address for the listener. Rather than simply talking in generalities, the introduction points to the issue for them and how it will affect their life and touch their own experience. This may be done through a story, a quote, a question, or in other ways.

SERMON GATES

There are, of course, many ways sermons can be introduced. Some have called the introduction the gateway into the sermon. These gateways can take an endless variety of routes. I will suggest a few, but you can cite many others as well. A preacher is deadly dull who begins every sermon the same way.

One Sentence. Sometimes the introduction may be only one sentence. Kelly Miller Smith began his sermon entitled "The Search" with a sentence: "The search is on."[40] He acknowledges, however, that for many the very reason for this search in life frequently eludes us. I began a sermon with the question: "Just who do you think you are?" The Pharisees asked Jesus. Then I moved into the questions about Jesus breaking the traditions of the Jews. The first sentence may set a tone, raise an issue, and offer a key or a sense of the direction of the sermon. Fosdick used to say, "Tell all you know in the first sentence." I think that is unrealistic but it can at least offer some suggestion of where you are headed.

A Textual Approach. The sermon could begin with a citation of the text in some way. But, if so, then do it with some more creativity than merely "Our text is…" In a sermon entitled "The View from Pisgah," Peter Gomes cites his text early in the sermon but introduces it with a question. "It seems unfair, don't you think?" Then he recounts that Moses had finished all the requirements but didn't graduate, and ends the five books of the Bible with the enigmatic remark of God which was his text. "I have let you see it with your eyes, but you shall not go over there" (Deuteronomy 14:4).[41] If you begin with the text put some picture frame around it.

A Newspaper Article. Robert McCracken, former minister at Riverside Church in New York City, tells about a clipping he had from *The New York Times* which made a perfect introduction to his sermon "The Wish to Escape" with the text "O for the wings of a dove that I might fly away and be at rest" (Psalm 55:6). The article recounted how a bus driver, who had been with his firm for sixteen years, took the wheel of his bus and instead of driving it back and forth in the Bronx as he had done week in week out for years, drove it right to Florida.[42] An article about a man who had killed a state trooper appeared recently in *the Richmond Times-Dispatch.* In the article the man who shot the trooper said that he did it because "God told me to do it." That article could introduce a sermon entitled: "What Kind of God Do We Worship?"

The Comics. The comics found in the daily newspaper can provide a rich source for sermons, especially the introductions. I have drawn frequently from *Peanuts, Blondie, Family Circus, For Better or Worse, Kudzu and Calvin and Hobbes* among others. The conversation between Lucy and Charlie Brown in one of the *Peanuts* comics would make a good introduction to a sermon entitled: "Facing Yourself." Lucy says to Charlie Brown, "The whole trouble with you is that you won't listen to the whole trouble with you." And isn't that the problem with all of us?

Historical Material. Fosdick introduces a sermon, "The Decisive Babies of the World," a Christmas sermon, with a reference to the English historian Sir Edward Shepherd Creasy's famous volume on *The Fifteen Decisive Battles of the World* published in 1851. After referring to the book, Fosdick then continues, "But now Christmas comes again, engaging the thought and warming the heart of multitudes around the globe, and it concerns not a decisive battle but a decisive baby. 'Unto us a child is born, unto us a son is given.'"[43] This introduction begs the listener to weigh which is more important: a battle or a baby.

A Provocative Question. Questions of all kinds can be raised at the onset of the sermon to indicate that this is the dilemma before the listeners this morning. In a series on "The Last Words from the Cross," I preached on John 19:30 under the title "The Triumphant Shout." The introduction began this way: "For six hours Jesus had hung upon the cross. He seemed to realize that the end was near, and with a loud shout he cried: 'It is finished!' But what was finished?"[44] Robert McCracken published a book of sermons, *Questions People Ask*, based on the problems and issues uppermost in the minds of modern men and women.[45] Think of the questions people ask: Is there a God? Can I find God? How can I become a Christian? Do we live after we die? Isn't being decent enough? Why did Jesus have to die? Many in our congregation struggle with such questions.

A Humorous or Amusing Incident. A humorous personal experience or some story you have read or heard can be used to introduce your sermon if the story genuinely relates to the central focus of your sermon. This is not permission for telling jokes. They rarely have their place in the pulpit. Fred Craddock is a master storyteller and many of his stories are humorous and make his point well and bear the listener into the sermon with merriment. Look, for example, at his sermons in *The Cherry Log Sermons* collection, and especially the sermon "At Random" or "Looking Around During the Prayer" in *The Collected Sermons of Fred B. Craddock.*[46]

Personal Experiences. Every preacher has numerous personal stories she can share that will be well received by the congregation. These, of course, should not be stories to make the preacher look good but genuine recollections that are relevant to the sermon and can introduce it effectively. Again Fred Craddock is a master at this, as is John Killinger. Killinger introduced a Christmas sermon by recounting a time he was looking in the window of a shop in Washington State which was filled with all kinds of the season's items although it was still summertime. On the corner of the front door was a sign that said: "Christmas Spoken Here." That became the title of his sermon.[47] This type of story can be as simple as recounting a conversation with someone. I introduced a sermon of Jesus washing the disciples' feet this way: "Recently, a church member told me that one of the most vivid memories that he had from his small rural church was the service of foot washing. I don't expect there are too many of us who have actually participated in such a service." Draw on your recollections. They are richer and fuller than you can imagine. But don't over use your personal stories.

These are only a few of the many sermon gates a preacher can use. Only your lack of reading, observation, and keeping records can blind you to the unlimited possibilities. Draw on plays, movies, TV, contemporary literature, magazines and newspapers, the special occasions of churches, conversations with people, classroom studies, conferences, Bible and devotional reading, observations of your family and nature, pastoral ministries and on and on.

THE CONCLUSION

I heard a woman say about her pastor's recent sermon, "He came to several good stopping spots but just could not stop. He simply went on and on way past the stopping place." Some ministers cannot conclude, while others end their sermons abruptly. A minister needs to learn how to conclude not just stop, to finish and not merely dribble off. Next to the introduction, the conclusion is one of the most vital parts of a sermon. It is not an appendage to the sermon but the necessary completeness of the sermon. The conclusion offers the preacher the last opportunity to communicate the final thrust of the central focus of the sermon, enabling the listener to discern the key thought in its clearest and sharpest focus; and the last moment to achieve the purpose for the sermon and connect the sermon's purpose with the congregation and to enable them to see the text's application to their own lives and the summons it issues to them for a decision or response.

THE PURPOSE OF THE CONCLUSION

The aim of the conclusion is to do the following: (1) Bring the sermon to a successful ending. (2) Make the central focus clear. (3) Invite the listener to discover the application of the sermon's focus or to arrive at their own conclusion. (4) Declare forcefully the application of the sermon's basic focus. (5) Issue a summons for a verdict, a commitment, a choice, a decision or some definite response. "A sermon has failed, indeed it has not been a sermon," declared H. H. Farmer in his Warrack Lectures, "unless it carries to the serious hearer something of a claim upon, or summons to, his will, to his whole being as this gathers itself together in the will." Continuing he concludes, "A sermon... should have something of the quality of a knock on the door."[48] The preacher might even use language in the conclusion like "I wish I could persuade you." I challenge you." "I invite you to consider." Or "I appeal to you."

SOME THINGS TO AVOID IN THE CONCLUSION

(1) Avoid humor in the conclusion. Humor is valuable in other places in the sermon but the conclusion is not the appropriate place for levity. *Rule*: Humor is useful but not in the conclusion. (2) Avoid ending the sermon the same way every week. *Rule*: Have variety in your conclusions. (3) Avoid adding new or different ideas in the conclusion. *Rule:* Conclude what the sermon's focus is. Don't add new ideas. (4) Make the conclusion brief. Avoid saying, "Just one more thing" or "Now in conclusion" several times. *Rule:* Be

brief in the conclusion. (5) Avoid distractions. Don't close your Bible or notes or reach for the bulletin to indicate that you are finished. *Rule:* Do not distract but focus.

The conclusion should be positive and appropriate to the theme of the sermon. It should also conclude the whole sermon and not just the final movement of the sermon. Seek to be clear not abstract, simple not complicated, practical not unrealistic. Let the central focus of the sermon be apparent in the conclusion whether it is an exhortation, encouragement, consolation, warning, invitation, challenge or something else.

Some Varieties of Conclusions

A Direct Declaration or Challenge. In a sermon called "The Hardest Blow of All" dealing with rejection, Ernest Campbell, former pastor at Riverside Church, New York City, concludes this way:

> It may very well be that some one of you is caught in the depression that rejection always brings. Anger and bitterness may seem the only way. I have three words for you. God loves you! Jesus understands you! The Church is ready to receive you as you are![49]

In a communion sermon, "Blessed Brokenness," about Jesus breaking bread with the two men he has been talking to on the Emmaus Road, Barbara Brown Taylor concludes in these words: "Take heart. This is not a ghost. Do not fear. You cannot lose him for good. This is the place he has promised to be, and this is the place he returns to meet us again and again. Risen Lord, be known to us in the breaking of bread."[50]

A Striking Question. John Claypool concludes a sermon on stewardship entitled "Joining the Church" with these words: "There is more at stake here than just pledging a budget. The issues of eternal destiny and whether or not the whole world will be blessed or neglected are at stake. This is a momentous occasion. What, then, will you do?"

William H. Willimon, formerly chaplain at Duke University and Methodist Bishop in Alabama, in a sermon "Harmless Hospitality" concludes in this manner: "'Behold, I stand at the door and knock,' Jesus said. Let's go ahead and let him in. You want to ask him in? What harm could he do?"[51]

An Illustration or Pictorial Image. Leslie Weatherhead, late minister at City Temple, London, England, concludes a sermon, "The Modern Christian and Sunday" with a personal story:

> Let me finish with one picture. Some time ago I was called to see an old man over eighty years of age who was dying and who was very frightened of death, as some old people are. And when, as tenderly as I could, I tried to talk to him about God and religion and the soul, he said, very bitterly and brokenly. Mumbling as he said the words, "I have led a very busy life. I have never had time for that sort of thing…" But he had had four thousand Sundays![52]

In a sermon entitled "A Church Like It Oughta Be" William Sloane Coffin, late minister at Riverside Church, New York City, concluded with this image:

> Yesterday, in the bottom of the ninth, the Mets proved true the saying that is written high above the bleachers of Shea Stadium: "Baseball like it oughta be."
>
> We're nowhere near the bottom of the ninth, and we don't need to hang out any sign. But let's be a church like it oughta be.[53]

I have mentioned only three types of conclusions. The varieties of sermon conclusions can be almost endless. They could include a resume or summary of the central focus, an appeal to the imagination of the listeners, the quoting of a poem or hymn, citing the text again, making a contrast (in keeping with the sermon's central focus), for example, moving from sin to salvation or from darkness to light, an encouragement or warning, or the conclusion may be missing with an invitation for the listeners to append their own. As one moves toward the conclusion, be sure to use a proper transition or connecting bridge words to the ending. Words like "And now"- "So"- "Thus"-"Therefore"- "Surely then" "Could it not be possible?" "You have traveled to this juncture; will you now go with me here?" This will keep the conclusion from being abrupt and bear the people with you.

PERSONAL OR GROUP QUESTIONS & REFLECTIONS

1. Discuss what you think constitutes an effective sermon introduction and conclusion.
2. What are some of the major things to avoid in introductions and conclusions?
3. Name some preachers you know who have captured your attention with their introductions. What was the factor about the introduction that caused this to happen?
4. Do you think a preacher should prepare the introduction and conclusion ahead of time or let the Spirit or inspiration of the moment determine them?
5. Discuss how you would introduce and conclude a sermon on the text where Jesus says, "I am the light of the world" (John 8:12).
6. Examine some of the sermons by someone like Fred Craddock or William Willimon and discuss how you think they introduced their sermons.

Are We Going Somewhere?

The Structure and Main Movements of the Sermon

A minister friend of mine told me that when he was on vacation recently, he went to hear a preacher on Sunday in a church near their beach house. He said the preacher's sermon reminded him of a cat chasing its tail. The preacher kept going around in circles like the cat pursuing its tail without the preacher or those of us in the congregation catching any point or direction where he might be trying to go. Preachers sometimes assume that they don't need any structure in their sermons. They simply try to wing it after reading the text. Unfortunately, this lack of sermon structure often visualizes the preacher as "jogging in place." The sermon seems to lack direction or movement. A lot of words are often spewed out, but they do not march to any particular drum beat. Sermon structure will help the preacher avoid the weakness of a sermon seemingly being depicted as "thrown together" without planning or design. Structure will help give the sermon design, focus, direction and organization.

The Importance of Structure

An architect projects the construction of a building by preparing blueprints to guide the contractor and construction crew. An engineer follows designs and plans to build a bridge or some other structure. A lawyer relies on law books for legal guidance; a musician follows the notes before her; athletes abide by rules to play a game correctly; a cook relies on recipes; a seamstress follows a pattern. Almost everyone follows some kind of standard to pursue their goal well. I believe this is true for preachers too. Good structure is essential for an effective sermon.

Drawing on Julian Huxley's image of "a sea animal essaying motion on land without a skeleton collapsing gelatinously," Halford Luccock, who was the professor of homiletics at Yale Divinity School for many years, in a picturesque way, advised his students in preaching classes that "The fear of the Lord is the beginning of wisdom in preaching, but the fear of gelatin also helps."[54] Preachers, he suggested, need to add the word "gelatinously" to their vocabulary as they prepare their sermons. Many sermons do indeed collapse gelatinously because of the lack of structure.

The traditional approach to creating a sermon structure has been to make an outline of the sermon with major and often minor sub-points. This conventional outline was Hegelian-like with three points depicted often as thesis, antithesis and synthesis with a poem at the end. The outline would sometimes follow the text, and on other occasions the outline would be based on the sermon's theme. In the past homileticians offered suggestions of dozens of kinds of outlines, such as ones that raise questions, classification outline, guessing games, examining the reflections of a diamond, exploring a problem, offering a rebuttal, a repeating rifle sequence, and on and on.[55]

Since the introduction of Fred Craddock's inductive approach to preaching, some contemporary professors of preaching have suggested that the process of sermon construction should more correctly be called "moves" rather than outlines. They do not see the sermon as a law brief or proposition to be analyzed rationally and spelled out or laid out in some legalistic fashion. David Buttrick has suggested that before preachers can develop their sermons they "must see what sermons are made of — namely a series of rhetorical units or moves. So we must study moves to see how they are shaped out of words and sentences and how, in turn, they form in the old shared consciousness we call a 'congregation.'"[56] Our task is to see how the text moves and how it takes life in the parishioners' lives.

Other teachers of preaching like Thomas Long, Fred Craddock, Eugene Lowry, Paul Scott Wilson and others have suggested various ways to express the movement of a sermon.[57] Whether one calls sermon structure "moves," "narratives," "forms" or whatever, they all acknowledge that some kind of "forms," shapes or patterns are essential for sermons. I personally think "moves" expresses better what the preacher is seeking to accomplish in the development of the sermon than the use of the word "outline."

There are advantages both for the preacher and the congregation for the preacher to have structure in the sermon. Let's examine some of those now.

ADVANTAGES OF SERMON STRUCTURE FOR THE PREACHER

Determines the Sermon's Direction. Without planning the sermon, the preacher can drift into a no man's land without focus or direction. She might spend her time "chasing rabbits." Once the text or theme is known and the central focus is clear, then the preacher can begin to formulate the direction of the sermon. Sometimes the movements of the sermon are clear from the text; on other occasions, they may be planned through reflection on the theme. Before the sermon can have "moves" for me, I often have to begin in an outline format exploring several options, rejecting others, revising my first thoughts, etc. before I can translate my thinking into "moves." This step allows you to determine the route you want to take, how you will organize your sermon, and gives you the freedom to revise it and develop your thought as you move down the path.

Focuses on the Theme. Structure will aid the preacher in keeping on the path the central focus has determined throughout the whole sermon. How many times have we heard preachers drift down side streets because they have lost or never had the sermon's focus clearly in mind? If the central focus of the sermon is "The redeeming grace of Jesus Christ on the cross," this focus should keep the sermon from drifting into a reflection of baptism, ecology, marriage, etc. Structure should keep you on track and guide you in exactly what you are trying to say.

Aids in the Proportion of the Sermon Movements. As the preacher is preaching the text, he should try to allow a proper proportion or balance in the various movements of the sermon. This may not always work because of the nature of the text, but can assist the preacher from spending too much time on a minor part of the text or discussing a problem and allowing no time to suggest the solution. I call this "elephant-phonic" preaching which focuses on the elephant's large trunk and body in description, problem discussion, etc. and offers only the "elephant's tail" as the diagnosis or remedy. For example, the preacher may spend too much time preaching about the nature of sin and offer only a scant moment for preaching about the grace and forgiveness of God. How many times have we heard a preacher say, "Oh, if I had more time I would say…?" What that reveals, of course, is poor planning of the sermon structure.

Provides Sign Markers Along Your Route. In the traditional outline, this would be depicted as "slots" or "pegs" on a board to lay out the plan of the sermon. But for "moves" in the sermon, the moves are more like sign markers on the road on which you are traveling. The sign posts help guide you but do not limit your movement or make it static. The preacher follows the growing and developing thought of the text as she concentrates on the central focus of the text as the sermon moves toward the conclusion.

Assists the Preacher in Remembering the Sermon. When the preacher is aware of the movements of the sermon and follows them in the delivering of the sermon, she will be able to remember the sermon better. This is especially true for preachers who preach without a manuscript. Throughout most of my ministry, I have preached without notes or a manuscript before me. Knowing the movements and sub-movements in the text and my transition from one movement to the next in my mind has enabled me to do this kind of preaching. Even if the preacher has notes with the movement themes before him, this will assist him in the delivery of the sermon.

Advantages for the Listener

More Intelligible. If the preacher's sermon has carefully planned structure, the congregation will be able to follow, understand and sense where the preacher is going with the message. Rather than words and sentences poorly thrown together and illustration that seem unconnected, structure can tie the sermon together in a "package" that is pleasing, shows order and movement and is aptly illustrated.

Maintains Attention. When the congregation is listening to the sermon, a person may pause for a moment in listening to the sermon and his mind may drift on to another matter or he may spend a moment reflecting on what the preacher has just said. If the preacher has carefully structured the sermon with good, clear movements, then when the hearer returns to listening, he will be able to continue following the movement of the sermon. Structure will help in keeping the attention of the listeners.

More Pleasing. The preacher needs to be aware of the attention curve of the listener when preaching the sermon. No one will listen without the mind drifting to some other thoughts arising to the surface as the preacher's words may elicit some other matter in the hearer's mind. There needs to be a psychological "break" for the listener, if she is to continuing listening. The movement from one movement to another may help provide this psychological break. It may also be done by the preacher relaxing momentarily, taking a breath and a slight pause between movements, and then inviting the congregation to journey further with him in the text's focus. Sometimes a change of pace, a variation in the intensity of one's delivery or a story or a pictorial image may help achieve this psychological pause or necessary emotional rhythm in listening.

More Memorable. Sermon structure with the movements clearly sensed or revealed will help the hearer to remember the sermon that has just been preached. The preacher needs to be careful here that she doesn't aim for "cuteness" which people will remember rather than substance. Leonard Griffith in a sermon on the Good Samaritan focuses on three philosophies of life in the parable. (1) The Robbers-"What's yours is mine, I'll take it." (2) The priest and Levite- What's mine is mine, I'll keep it." (3) The Samaritan-"What's mine is yours, I'll share it."[58] Effective moves will make the sermon hard to forget.

MOVES IN A SERMON'S STRUCTURE

In the traditional outline format the preacher would prepare his sermon with points labeled like I, II, III, IV or A, B, C, or D. Often there would be sub-points under the numbers like I. could have 1, 2, and 3 as sub-points under the main number and so on through the outline. Long says the newer inductive approach is composed of "a series of small segments, or movements which building cumulatively toward a climactic 'Aha.'"[59] Transitional words are used to connect the smaller moves or units. Craddock suggests that this form is really a "problem solving activity" that invites the listener to participate in the process to determine what the text means for us today and reach a point that they see the claim the text has on them personally.[60] The larger movements arise at their best out of the movement of the text itself.

Even in inductive formatting sub-movements are parts of the process. These sub-moves can offer steps under the larger move that carry the listener to the next major movement. They are made clear to the listener often with transition words or phrases like "However one might think otherwise," "Nevertheless," "In another sense," "And yet," "It seems this but maybe that," "You have thought about this, but have you considered this possibility?" "Go further and think with me," "That seems to be true but what if this were true?" Other transition words might include: "such as again," "still again," "another thing," "not only this but that," or "on the other hand." Connectors like "therefore," "however," "moreover" can be used.

Phrases like "Having said that, another side might be considered;" "Would you agree with me that this is possible?" "Put that on hold and come with me to consider." "If you think that verse is striking, note the way Paul continues."

Transitions form bridges to the next move in the listeners' mind. Each movement is designed to carry you toward the sermon's conclusion where the listener is to make a response in the light of the meaning of the sermon text for him or her. The sermon is merely a "noisy gong or a clanging cymbal," (1 Cor. 1:1, NRSV) to use the Apostle Paul's depiction, if there is no invitation for the listener to be addressed or challenged by the sermon.

Good sermon movements will be filled with vivid images, metaphors, stories, narratives, and pictures. They will not try to solve all problems but maybe raise some; disturb as well as comfort; warn as well as encourage; confront as well as invite; teach as well as practice; serve as well as receive. The moves should evoke anticipation, discovery, actualization, hope and realization. Fred Craddock reminds the preacher that "the movement of your sermon be primary, not the structure." The structure may not be remembered, he notes, but what the movement sounds like in the delivery of the sermon is the important thing not what it looks like on paper. Anticipation in the movement will keep the preacher alive in the sermon and carry the listeners with you as well.[61]

The last thing the preacher needs to do is to "dangle the skeleton" in the sermon before the congregation. Announcing the movement by one, two and three, I do not believe, is helpful. Nor do I believe it is wise to pass out to the congregation the "outline" of your sermon ahead of time or flash it in full on a screen before the congregation. This removes the surprise and anticipation elements which are essential to good preaching.

A VARIETY OF SERMON MOVEMENTS

Biblical preaching, Craddock attests, "asks not only what the text says but *how* it says it. Instead of moving away from the Bible to enliven your preaching, move in closer and see how the Bible does it."[62] The many forms in the Bible can guide the preacher in determining the form or movement of her sermon. Here are a few examples:

A One Sentence Text. Sometimes one text can offer enough resources that the preacher can faithfully preach it. Think of such verses as John 3:16, Philippians 4:13, and Ephesians 2:5. Karl Barth drew on one verse from Ephesians 2:8 and his moves are clearly seen:

1. ***By grace*** you have been saved.
2. By grace ***you*** have been saved.
3. By grace you ***have been saved****.*[63]

I preached a sermon entitled "Christians Unashamed" based on the one verse from Romans 1:16. My movements followed the text in this way:

1. Many bear a sense of shame.
2. Not ashamed of the Gospel.
3. Not ashamed of the power of God.
4. Not ashamed of the power of God for salvation.
5. Not ashamed of salvation as a gift for everyone.[64]

Two Contrasting Truths. Frederick W. Robertson preached a sermon entitled "The Irreparable Past" based on Matthew 14:41-42. The first part of the sermon was negative and the second was positive: 1. "The irreparable past." 2. "The available future."[65] Another contrasting sermon might be based on Luke 18:9-14 about the Pharisee and the Publican. 1. The Danger of self-satisfaction. 2. The beauty of Christian humbleness. The brevity and conciseness of these movements can make the focus of the sermon clear.

The Question Movement. The preacher examines the text and lifts a question from it, or questions arise from it as movements. Charles Wesley used this approach in a sermon "The Scripture Way of Salvation" based on Ephesians 2:8.

1.   What is salvation?

2. What is the faith whereby we are saved?
3. How are we saved by it?

A question sermon might be based on John 3:16 entitled "The Extent of God's Love." The questions might be as follows:

1. Who extended this love?
2. To whom was this love directed?
3. What did God give to show God's love?
4. What happens to those who believe?

Expanding the Text. The movement of this sermon grows out of or builds on the previous movement or carries the thought to another level or appeal. The Scottish preacher James Stewart has a sermon "The Triumphant Adequacy of Christ" based on Romans 15:29 "I am sure that, when I come unto you, I shall come in the fullness of the blessing of the gospel of Christ." Notice the expansion of the moves:

1. I am coming to you with Christ.
2. I am coming to you with the gospel of Christ
3. I am coming to you with the blessing of the gospel of Christ.
4. I am coming to you with the fullness of the blessing of the gospel of Christ.[66]

An Exposition of the Text. The preacher might select a text like Psalm 23 and follow the moves of the text to include 1. The assurance of the presence of the Shepherd. 2. The restoration of our soul. 3. The security and healing of God. 4. A feast of grace. 5. Comfort through the valley of death. Paul's description of "the armor of God" in Ephesians 6:10-17 could be a sermon in which the preacher could draw upon each piece of the armor and note its meaning for the Christian life today.

Highlight Three Movements. Sometimes the text may fall naturally into three movements and the preacher can follow those moves. For example, the lectionary passages from Galatians 4:1-7 might focus on its first movement on the law as "custodian" or "guardian." (Gal. 4:2). The second movement addresses the One who came to "redeem those who were under the law" (Gal.4:5). The final movement affirms the new status of what it means to be a child of God through Christ's redemption. (Gal. 4:5). Another lectionary lesson, Psalm 29, falls naturally into three movements. The first movement summons the heavenly angels to worship (Ps. 29:1-2). The second movement contains the main thrust of the passage in its majestic and powerful affirmation of God as revealed in the violent thunderstorms. God's glory is presented in a sevenfold proclamation of power (Ps. 29:3, 7). The last movement turns to the calm after the storm (Ps. 29:10-11).

Since there are many varieties in the forms found in the Bible, the preacher needs to study them carefully and incorporate as many as she can in her sermon structure. The Bible is a rich storehouse and the preacher needs to draw abundantly from its vast resources for designing sermons. Draw from the well of the Bible; it will never run dry.

Personal or Group Questions & Reflections

1. How can the preacher be assured that his sermon will have direction and movement?
2. What are some ways the preacher can learn how to design and craft her sermon?
3. Examine a passage like Mark 8:34-35; John 12:1-8 or Philippians 2:5-8 and show how you would structure the sermon and explain how you determined your moves.
4. Suggest other possible sermon movements.
5. Do you feel that Craddock's inductive approach is well-taken in sermon construction or do you feel that the traditional outline method is still valid or at least an option?

Painting a Picture:

The Importance of Illustrations

Since childhood most of us have loved stories. They have not only entertained us, prompted our imagination, taken us on distant journeys, taught us about magical people and places, but they have inspired and enlightened us. It is no wonder that people say that what they remember most about a preacher's sermon is the stories. They may not follow our movements, catch our explanation of the secrets of the text, or follow our theological thinking, but they won't forget the stories or illustrations we use to clarify what we are trying to say. The "giants" of the pulpit like Henry Ward Beecher, Charles Spurgeon, Harry Emerson Fosdick, John Killinger, Gardner Taylor, Peter Gomes, Barbara Brown Taylor, and Fred Craddock have all been master story-tellers. They knew and used effectively the power of illustrations.

WHAT IS AN ILLUSTRATION?

The word "illustration" literally means "to bring light" or "to throw light or luster" upon a thought or subject. Illustrations may take many shapes from stories, pictorial images, analogies, metaphors, examples, figures of speech, quotations to many other depictions. Homileticians in the past have often characterized illustrations as being what "windows" are to houses — they let in some light on the subject.

Thomas Long has criticized this approach, which was based on the belief that a sermon was a "house" built on logic and reasoning. This is a didactic or rationalistic conception of preaching. This view of illustrations seems to imply that the rest of the sermon does not clearly convey the message. Long argues, instead, that a sermon is like a doorway that opens into a larger room of understanding and experience, one that is wide enough that all the listeners can pass through it.[67]

WHY USE ILLUSTRATIONS?

We follow the Master Teacher. The preacher today cannot find a better model for using illustrations in preaching than Jesus himself. "With many such parables," Mark writes, "he (Jesus) spoke the word to them as they were able to hear it; he did not speak to them except in parables." (Mark 4:33-34). New Testament scholars have suggested that Jesus taught from thirty to sixty parables with many other uses of pictorial language.[68] T. W. Manson has argued, however, that the true parable of Jesus "is not an illustration to help one through a theological discussion; it is rather a mode of religious experience."[69] Kenneth Bailey writes that Jesus' use of parables, rather than giving an abstract statement and following it with a clarifying illustration, is "a concrete/dramatic form of theological language that presses the hearer to respond." They are revealing the nature of the kingdom of God or demonstrating how a person of the kingdom should live.[70] What better understanding for the use of an illustration can a preacher have than this: the illustration presses the hearer to be made aware of the kingdom of God and respond to how he or she is to live as a Christian in that kingdom?

Communicates the Central Focus of the Sermon. If an illustration is trying to make the listener in some way aware of the kingdom of God, then the preacher will be focusing on the central focus of the sermon and not trying to let in a bit of light on a dimension of it. This way the listener is carried forward in the movement of the sermon to the conclusion which summons a response of some kind from the listener.

Persuasion. This is a part of the central focus of the sermon moving the listener to respond to the message. Through a story or a picturesque image, the preacher may be able to lead the listener to walk through the door which has been opened into the wider path of commitment or service. The ultimate goal is not merely to share an idea but to persuade the listener to respond to the gospel message. An effective illustration can serve this function.

Clarification. Since people think today more in a picture-like way with television and the movies, illustrations can make the central focus clearer. "Storytelling is something we can all do," Charles Rice reminds us, "it is an art to which we all readily respond."[71] People may respond more readily and see the meaning of the sermon more clearly with a story or some type of pictorial image. "The human mind is not, as philosophers would have you think, a debating hall," MacNeile Dixon wrote in his Gifford Lectures, "but a picture gallery."[72] The listener may get the thrust of the sermon far better through an illustration than through sound argument, though sound thinking is indeed essential. The illustration can provide the "thinking pause" when the listener pauses with the illustration to allow her mind to reflect, or catch up with the preacher or run ahead some in her thinking to grasp the focus more clearly.

Sustains Interest. No matter how effective a preacher may be in laying out the central focus of his sermon, if it is done only by stacking ideas in a row like stacking bricks, the listener will have a hard time maintaining interest or, I believe, maintaining attention. A story or some kind of picture or image will carry the thought further more effectively. Arguing additionally how people think, Dixon states:

Metaphor is the essence of religion and poetry. Take the similes, the figurative speech out of the world's poetry and you reduce it to commonplace. Remove the metaphors from the Bible, and its living spirit vanishes, its power over the heart melts utterly away. The prophets, the poets, the leaders of men are all of them masters of imagery, and by imagery they capture the human soul.[73]

Translates Theological/Biblical Language into Practical Imagery. A common complaint from lay persons is that their pastor preaches in a language, biblical and theological, that is not intelligible to them. The pastor has to work at translating the biblical and theological language into the common language of her listeners. The philosopher Schopenhauer used to say, "Think like a philosopher but speak like a man in the street." I was attending a Bible conference several years ago and following a lecture by a distinguished theologian, who delivered his lecture in abstract, pedantic, philosophical language. A friend came up to me and asked: "What in the world was all that ------- about?" Just as he could not understand that lecture because of the abstract language used, so many sermons are lost to the listeners by abstract, theological language. Illustrations of whatever kind may help translate the central focus of the sermon for the listener.

Provide a Necessary Psychological Pause. It is hard to maintain the attention of the listener without some kind of psychological pause so the listener is allowed to catch up, reflect or analyze the sermon movement thus far. An illustration can provide that necessary psychological pause. It is a change of pace from the regular flow of the presentation which is introduced by some kind of transition phrase or sentence like "However," or Now again," or "Going further," or "Maybe like ...," followed by a pause, and then the preacher moves into the illustration. This change of pace allows the necessary, refreshing pause.

Affords a Way to Remember. As I stated earlier, most lay persons and even preachers say what they remember most about a sermon is the illustrations. Illustrations without question make the sermon more memorable. They provide a mental basket for the listener to carry away the central focus of the sermon, if the illustration does its work appropriately. "Theology and ethics and anything else worth preaching may and perhaps must be stated in careful argument," Henry Mitchell argues in his Lyman Beecher Lectures. "But it won't reach the whole person until it is translated into moving and graphic art and symbol — word pictures and narration."[74] This narration, word picture, symbol, art form, etc. not only arrests the attention and understanding of the listeners but helps them remember what has been communicated through the sermon. Mitchell goes so far as to say: "If you have an idea that can't be translated into a story or a picture, don't use it."[75] The preacher has to remember, if she expects her people to remember the sermon, that people think analogically not logically. Hence, we note the power of parables, stories, and word images. Every preacher has to learn to tell stories and "paint pictures" for his or her congregation.

PRINCIPLES FOR EFFECTIVE ILLUSTRATIONS.

First, *illustrations need to be understandable.* If I tell an illustration about the Powhite Parkway, a toll road in Richmond, Virginia, and do not explain the nature of that road to my listeners who may live in another city and are unfamiliar with that road, then the story would be meaningless and no help at all in illuminating the sermon. The illustration must relate to the experience of the congregation.

Second, *an illustration should be applicable.* When the listener hears the illustration, the application should be apparent. If you have to explain your illustration, it's not worthy of telling. It has to stand on its own two feet without your having to prop it up with something else. It casts light on the pathway ahead but does not call attention to itself.

Third, *the illustration should be authentic.* If you get an illustration from another preacher or some other source, acknowledge the person by name or at least say "as a noted preacher or novelist has said." Do not claim somebody else's material or experience as your own. That is dishonest. A minister called me one day about a preacher he had heard using an illustration in his sermon that he claimed was his own experience, but he remembered reading it in a book I had written. He asked me if I got it from this preacher. I told him I had not, and that it was indeed my personal experience. This kind of dishonesty in preaching will cause people to question not only the preacher's integrity but, unfortunately, it might lead some to question the authenticity of our faith.

Fourth, an *illustration should be believable*. This means the preacher should not use an illustration that isn't accurate in its historical, literary, scientific, religious or biographical facts. Avoid telling a story that sounds unbelievable unless you can document or authenticate it in some concrete way with a different source. Someone has said that if preachers were hooted down when they told stories that were known to be untrue or outrageously exaggerated or blaringly inaccurate, we would have shorter sermons.

Fifth, *illustrations should be fresh*. Avoid telling time-worn stories that you gather off the internet or out of canned illustration books. Many of these illustrations may have been used dozens of times and heard by the congregation before. If the preacher does wide reading of novels, theology and other books, she will open the gate to many fresh ideas. Make a rule for yourself as a preacher that you will not offer stale bread to your congregation. Instead offer freshly baked loaves from your own oven of reading and experience. It will greatly enrich your preaching and your congregation will be immensely grateful.

Sixth, *an illustration should enliven the imagination*. If the illustration is effective, it should invite the listener to travel with the preacher into the story or imagery and explore the message for one's self. How is this narrative or imagery his or hers and how are they addressed by it and what is it calling them to do? Does this image summon the listener to imagine his life in a different or new perspective? Fiction often carries us in our imagination to many different realms. Hopefully, a good illustration will beckon the listener to such a journey. After all isn't our faith an imaginative leap into the unknown grasp of God? Jesus said "the kingdom of God is like…" and enters our imagination. "When I speak about my humanity," Barbara Brown Taylor proclaims about her preaching, "I want my listeners to recognize their own. When I say 'I' from the pulpit, I want them to say, 'me too.'" Continuing she writes:

> The sermon is no place for a virtuoso performance; it is a place for believers to explore together their common experience before God. The stories I tell from the pulpit are not just "my"

stories but "our" stories, which are God's stories too. The stool of my sermon rests evenly on those three legs. If any one of them is missing (or too long or too short), the whole thing will wobble and fall.[76]

The stories — illustrations — preachers tell are not for entertainment, but they are invitations into the stories about God, life and meaning. We enter them through the gate of our own imagination to be addressed by God.

Seventh, *an illustration must be appropriate with the central focus.* An illustration that has nothing to do in assisting to communicate the central focus should not be used no matter how good it is. Don't add trivial or additional stories just to fill up time or because they lighten the load of the sermon or are simply pleasing to be heard or will merely bring levity without embellishing the sermon. The use of such illustrations may only serve to cheapen or diminish the sermon's movement. Always strive to keep your central focus of the sermon paramount in your entire sermon's structure, especially in your use of illustrations.

VARIETIES OF SOURCES FOR ILLUSTRATIONS

Thomas Long has chosen to list sermon illustrations under three basic figures of speech: analogy, example, and metaphor.[77] Although I believe there is a lot of truth in what he says, I think it is helpful to list a variety of possibilities. The list below is not inclusive since the possibilities are almost endless.

The Bible. From Genesis to Revelation the Bible abounds with stories about Abraham, Jacob, Moses, Daniel, Sara, Esther, David, Peter, James and John, Mary and Martha, Paul and numerous others. Their lives are rich with lessons. The parables in the Old Testament as well as the parables of Jesus in the New Testament are rich for imagery. Sometimes a reference to a biblical character, parable or proverb or something else may be a fitting illustration.

Literature. Novels, short stories and plays offer a vast resource for illustrations. A preacher should not read them simply for that reason but for enjoyment and personal growth. Nevertheless, while reading them illustrations will leap out at you. Make notation of them in your journal or on your computer so you can use them later. From one of Dostoevsky's novels, the Russian author describes a scene where a man is standing before a painting of the crucifixion. "Don't look at that picture, you fool," another character cries, "Don't you know a man can lose his faith by looking at that picture?" "Yes," the man replied. "That is what is happening to me." I used this story in a sermon on "The Scandal of the Cross." Another story about the cross came from a novel by Joseph Hocking in a novel entitled *The Trampled Cross*. A British soldier has been captured by Arabs during some desert fighting. The Arabian chief took two sticks and made a sign of the cross, laid them in the sand and told the soldier, "There is the symbol of your faith. Trample on it, and we shall let you go free."

Autobiography and biography. I encourage the preacher always to be reading some biography or autobiography. Some recent ones I have read are Barbara Brown Taylor, *Leaving Church*, Henlee Hulix Barnette, *A Pilgrimage of Faith*, Gardner C. Taylor, *Submissions to the Dean*, E. Glenn Hinson, *A Miracle of Grace*, and Harvey Cox, *Just as I Am*. This material will give you personal information about their lives and much guidance in sermon growth.

Personal Experience. From the pastoral experience of everyday encounters with our church members and others, endless stories and quotes will emerge for your sermons. Simple ones like an experience I had with a group of boys and girls in our church sanctuary one day. One of the youngsters in the group as we walked around in the sanctuary paused and looked at me and asked: "Hey, Mr. Pastor, what goes on under this big roof?" Soon that question became the introduction and title to a sermon I did on worship. On another occasion I sat across the table for lunch in a fast food place from a man who was in a low mood that day in his life. "Does what happens in church," he asked me, "make any real difference in the lives of any of our church members?" This became an illustration in a sermon I did on "the Fellowship of the Church." Sometimes we may need to get permission to use the quote or illustration. Be careful not to embarrass other persons, especially if you draw a story from your own family life.

The Comics. I have notebooks filled with comics that I have collected from newspapers and magazines, especially *Peanuts*. I also have many of the special publications of the *Peanuts* comics by Charles Schulz. One I remember pictures Snoopy sitting on his dog house shivering in the cold and Charlie Brown saying: "You know, we should do something about that. He looks cold and hungry. Let's go over and help him." So he walks over and pats Snoopy on the head and says: "Be warmed, be fed, be comforted." Then he walks off and leaves him shivering in the cold. That story is straight out of the *Epistle of James* (2:17) and is ready made to be told.

Quotations. Used sparingly quotations can add richness and sparkle sometimes to our sermons. I remember seeing the play, *To Culebra* about the construction of the Suez Canal. Speaking to his son one day, Ferdinand Delesseps, who built the canal, told him, "You must remember that the pessimists are the spectators of life." Another short quote came from a new member of my church at St. Matthews when the man said: "I don't know when I have ever been so excited about a church before." This can be a rallying cry to call others to arise up and serve Christ in the church. Your reading will also give you an abundance of quotations. But use them sparingly.

Use your imagination and create an illustration. Frederick Buechner is a master at this. Every preacher should invest some thought to drawing on his imagination to create some story or pictorial language in sermons. Here is a parable I created and used in a sermon on "A New Commandment of Love" from 1 John 4:7-12.

> *One day there was a man who was lonely and had no sense of meaning in life. But he heard that people in the Cube had love and life. So one day he entered the Cube, and he experienced ecstatic joy and love. His life was changed. For many years his life in the Cube was wonderful. But then one day he began to hear tones of disharmony, dissatisfaction, and criticism by those*

inside the Cube. Some didn't like the color of the Cube. Some didn't like the size of the Cube. Others didn't like the shape of the Cube. Still others began to say that the Cube was too hot or too cold. There were those who didn't like the music in the Cube. It was too loud, too soft, too familiar, or too unfamiliar. Others were critical of the Cube leader. They didn't like some of the things he said or did.

Soon dissension began to break out in the group. Some declared, "There is only one way to understand the Cube. You have to believe in right angles to understand the meaning of the Cube." Others said, "Oh, no. It is the straight line that determines the correct understanding of the Cube." Still others declared, "Any angles are O.K." Soon little cubes were built inside the big Cube. These little cubes were established with each cube declaring that its cube had unique insights into what the Cube was really like, "My cube is more correct than your cube," each declared.

Then another more vocal group arose. "The only way you can ever understand the Cube," they avowed, "is by knowing the square. Only those who follow the square book can be real members of the Cube. It is only those who read and interpret the square book squarely who are members of the Cube. These persons have to wear square hats, sit in square holes, follow square rules, and think squarely. They must listen to square talks by square, male preachers. Only male square preachers can really understand and explain the meaning of the Cube for the rest of us. Women are to serve the square men."

Unfortunately, this division continued for a long time. Then one day the One, who had founded the Cube appeared in their midst, and he said to the people: "You have made me very sad. I built this Cube on a foundation of love. I laid down my life in love for you, and what I told you to do was to love one another. I told you that was all you needed to do." All of the smaller cube builders were very ashamed. They began to dismantle their cubes and harmony returned to the Cube again. Joy and love were once more experienced in the Cube.

Then one day some of those outside of the Cube saw the love that those in the Cube had for each other, and they asked if they could come into the Cube and share in that love. They, too, wanted to be a part of such love. The members of the Cube pointed these persons to the Founder of the Cube, who had taught them to love in this extraordinary way. This way of love surpasses all words and descriptions. He or she that hath ears to hear let him or her hear the meaning of this parable.[78]

Illustration Books. Illustration books are not the best resource for preachers, but they are better sources than not using any illustrations in the sermon. For preachers who are learning to preach, some of these books may be helpful, if one does not become dependent on them. I have to confess that I have found some helpful material in the past in sources like the three volumes of *A Reader's Notebook* by Gerald Kennedy, Charles L. Wallis *Speaker's Resources from Contemporary Literature, A Treasury of Sermon Illustrations* and *Speakers' Illustrations for Special Days* and *Halford Luccock Treasury*, edited by Robert Luccock. I am sure that none of these are still in print and many of the illustrations are dated. Since I have not used any of these sources for many years, I am not familiar with ones that may be newer. There are, of course, sources on the internet as well. Remember others draw from that source as well. Homileticians usually warn against using them, and that is correct to a point, but a busy pastor sometimes may have to dig into such materials. It is without question better to build your own files. Today mine are running over with years of accumulation. Your file can be too if you work at it continuously.

Other sources are plentiful for the preacher. Illustrations can be found in newspapers, periodicals, history, science, art, nature, sports, music, social and political life, anecdotes by others, sermon books by noted preachers — everywhere. Read widely, observe carefully, listen with a homiletical ear and record faithfully and you will always have a vast tool chest of illustrative material.

PERSONAL OR GROUP QUESTIONS & REFLECTIONS

1. How would you define illustration? Give some examples of good illustrations.
2. What constitutes effective illustrations?
3. Discuss some sources where you have found illustrations. Which ones have been most resourceful for you?
4. Have you ever created any of your own? What were they like?
5. Discuss your use of personal experiences as illustrations. What are some dangers of using personal stories?
6. Have you found illustration books or the internet helpful in finding good illustrations? What are some of their disadvantages?
7. Do you think it is important to give credit for your source when you use an illustration?

Out of Your Mouth:

The Oral Delivery of the Sermon

When I taught preaching at seminary, the students used to complain that preaching their sermon in homiletics class was the most anxiety driven thing they had to do in seminary. To be evaluated by one's peers is indeed a daunting undertaking. It was intimidating to preach and know that you are being evaluated by your fellow students and your professor. Because the classes I taught were large, often too large, the student had only two opportunities to preach in a semester. It was always pleasing to hear the second sermon and note the progress the student had made after studying and being critiqued. After seminary, if the preacher is in a parish ministry, he will be faced every week with the responsibility of standing before a congregation of persons from every walk of life. Whether she likes it or not, she will be evaluated by her listeners. The anxiety of standing before a congregation seldom totally disappears, and maybe it shouldn't, in the light of the awesome claim of speaking a word from God.

Before one dares to stand in that holy place and preach, we have emphasized the necessity of careful preparation. No delivery can erase sloppy preparation. The final test, of course, of any sermon is not what is on a piece of paper, but whether or not the preacher can actually orally deliver the sermon. The final assessment is in the delivery. "The preacher enhances or fails to enhance the effectiveness of the sermon," Charles Dupier observes, "by the manner in which it is delivered."[79] Here the preacher wins or loses in communicating his sermonic truth. All that the preacher has done up to this point will help or hurt. But the proof of the prepared word will be seen in the table set before the congregation. The congregation will come to this table and be fed or leave un- der- nourished.

When a sermon is "delivered," it is not simply the minister unloading what is on his mind as he speaks, rather, by telegraphing the message in such a way that it is lodged in the mind and hearts of the listeners, it challenges them to respond to the spoken word. Remember, a sermon is not really a sermon until it is proclaimed in a collected assembly. "A sermon is not a sermon until it is heard," Roger Van Harn declares. "Listeners finish the sermon by letting it into their lives — or sometimes by pulling hard on it to get it there."[80]

FACTORS THAT MAY AFFECT SERMON DELIVERY

The Conditions of the Church Sanctuary. Although some church architecture is beautiful in its design, it may not be conducive for effective preaching. The minister may be far removed from the congregation which sits at a great distance from the pulpit and can hardly see the minister. The sound system may also be poor and the people cannot hear you well. In some churches police and truck drivers' calls come in on the sound system. Crying babies and chil- dren moving around in the aisles can be distracting to the preacher and congregation. Poor attendance in a half-filled sanctuary can affect the preacher's mood.

The Preacher's Physical Condition. If the preacher has not had enough sleep the night before, has eaten too much or not at all, or has been consumed by too much pastoral or administrative re- sponsibilities the week before, her preaching may be drastically influenced. If the preacher's voice is hoarse or weak or he has a sore throat because of a cold, his preaching will not be up to the best of his expectations. If the minister is depressed because of personal problems or from problems or criticism in the church, he won't be able to perform as he wants.

Lack of Preparation. When a minister has not prepared her sermon well, that will affect the delivery. As someone has said, the best delivery cannot save a poor sermon without content. Before the preacher can say it well, she has to have prepared something well to say. It is evident when the preacher is struggling for something to say, that he has not done his "homework." You can't deliver what you don't have. Be prepared.

Your Beginning Can Affect Your Delivery. The preacher should enter the pulpit with a sense of expectance. Your attitude should communicate that you are anticipating that the congregation will listen. Pause a moment and allow the listeners to prepare to listen. Just as a horse knows if the rider is accustomed to riding, a congregation can sense whether or not the preacher knows her business of preaching or not. Begin slowly in a conversational tone, not like you are addressing a crowd in a football stadium. If the preacher begins too abruptly or senses he has lost the attention of the congregation already, it will be difficult to recover and go forward very effectively.

Nervousness. Even veteran preachers will confess that they still have some nervousness when they stand up to speak. After you begin, hopefully, this will subside like an athlete before a game. Good preparation will also help slash some of the edge off. Concentrate on your message and have confidence that the congregation has your best interest in mind and will undergird you with their prayers. Severe nervousness will obliviously curtail your effectiveness. If it continues, seek help from an experienced older minister or from a speech teacher.

FIVE METHODS OF SERMON DELIVERY

I believe there are basically five ways sermon are delivered. Some ministers use a combination of these, and others have followed one particular method most of their ministry. I will note the advantages and disadvantages of each.

Impromptu Preaching. This style of preaching comes from one who has made little or no preparation and says that he will simply let the Holy Spirit guide him while he is preaching on Sunday. Another may read selectively and says she will preach out of the overflow. These preachers read a passage of Scripture and off they go speaking off the top of their head. That kind of preaching has given preaching a bad name and has turned many away from the church. A group of ministers was discussing their sermon preparation methods and one in the group said he simply stood in the pulpit and let the Spirit guide him. Another minister, without regard for the other minister's pomposity or feelings, was bold to say: "Yes. I have heard Brother Smith preach and I cannot believe that the Holy Spirit is so boring, trite and repetitious as he is." That is often the conclusion of many to that kind of preaching.

I recall that on a few rare occasions, I dared to enter the pulpit unprepared. The message I received from the Holy Spirit was: "Bill Tuck, you have been unnecessarily too busy or too lazy this week. So, wing it on your own this morning." Why should any preacher assume that the only place the Spirit can address the preacher is in the pulpit? I have found that the Spirit guides my sermon preparation more efficiently in my study than any place else. Then when I enter the pulpit, the Spirit may lead me in a different way than I have prepared but that is rare. I made a vow never to enter the pulpit unprepared. Someone might try to speak of some advantages of this method, but I see only arrogance, laziness, disregard of prayerful, Spirit-guided preparation and shallowness as looming reasons to avoid this method, if the preacher has any integrity.

Memorizing the Sermon. Some few preachers have memorized their written sermon and recited it before the congregation. Few have the kind of memory where this would be possible. The advantages are evident: the preacher can look at the congregation while he preaches and does not have to use notes. But think of the disadvantages: (1) it takes a lot of time to memorize the sermon. (2) The preacher may appear like a child or actor who is simply reciting a script. (3) She may stare at the back wall not to get distracted by the people. (4) He could appear stiff, artificial or perfunctory. (5) There could be a memory block and he forgets where he is in the sermon. (6) If it is a good "performance," is it a call for applause? I personally feel few ministers should ever attempt this method unless they are professional actors.

Preaching from Notes. In this method the preacher may write the manuscript out in full or simply make extensive notes for the sermon. What he takes into the pulpit is the outline of his major movements of thought with the minor moves listed under the major like:

I. Major   II. Second major

  1. Minor   1. Second minor

  2. Minor   2. Second minor

She might include under the appropriate movement an illustration and a quotation, if one is being used. The movement may be written in a full sentence or a brief summation to help with the memory. The *advantages* are obvious. (1) The preacher will not forget what he is saying because the notes assist him. (2) The illustrations and quotations are in hand. (3) The notes make clear the movement of the sermon and the preacher can follow them. (4) The notes give the preacher a greater sense of confidence and support. Some of the *disadvantages* might include: (1) if the minister only prepares notes, the preparation may be sketchy and incomplete. (2) Eye contact may be lost if the preacher is too dependent on her notes. (3) Sometimes the preacher calls too much attention to the notes on the pulpit and seems to get distracted by them. (4) The notes may be arbitrary and too slight to guide the preacher well.

Reading the Sermon from a Complete Manuscript. The minister carefully prepares his sermon and when he preaches, he reads the manuscript to the congregation. In the early church this was rarely done but in recent years has become more popular. One preacher once said that he had to write out what he was going to say otherwise he might never stop. Notice some *advantages* of this approach:

(1) the preacher is assured of saying what she wants to because it's written out in full in front of her. (2) You won't forget because you have the complete manuscript. (3) With the manuscript you can be more accurate and clear because you have worded it carefully. (4) Since the time was spent on preparing the manuscript, the preacher will not have to spend much time in planning the sermon delivery. (5) Reading the manuscript allows the preacher to be more relaxed and not have to worry about what comes next or will she miss a point or movement. (6) Reading is much easier on the preacher's nerves than the other methods.

Let me mention some *disadvantages* of this method. (1) Most of the advantages mentioned are for the preacher and not the listening congregation. (2) Few ministers can read a manuscript well. They get lost in the manuscript and focus too much on what they have written. (3) Reading the manuscript causes most ministers to lose all eye contact with the congregation. (4) Even reading may not remove all nervousness, and as I mentioned before, some nervousness is probably good for the preacher. (5) Some preachers become so dependent on reading that they cannot say anything effectively before their congregation without reading it. (6) The minister may be so involved with his manuscript that he loses all contact with the people to whom he is speaking. (7) Congregations say that the reading of the sermon by the pastor is the most disliked practice of all the ways to deliver a sermon.

Through the many years of listening to sermons, I have heard only a few ministers I thought read their sermons effectively and did not call the listener's attention to the actual reading of the sermon. The Scottish Washington, D. C. preacher, Peter Marshall, was recognized with this special gift. The late Carlyle Marney of Myers Park Baptist Church in Charlotte, North Carolina was a powerful preacher. His deep base voice, inflections, pauses, profound word usage and theological depth could be spellbinding. He could read it in such a way that you did not sense he was indeed reading it. But few preachers can do this. Most preachers read the manuscript in such a way as to put the listeners to sleep. Reading the manuscript by most preachers presents a handicap for the congregation.

The alternative to reading the manuscript is to preach it. Ministers like George Buttrick, Leonard Griffith and David H. C. Read prepared a manuscript and would read it over several times on several days before they preached it before Sunday and only looked at it in the pulpit but did not read it. Most listeners did not see that as reading it. The preacher can have the manuscript in front of her but not read it word for word but glance at occasionally it as if it were your notes. Rehearse the sermon enough times before you preach it so that you do not have to read it, and you can follow its movements without losing all eye contact with the congregation. This way you can put more energy into the sermon, and the congregation will appreciate it much better. But that means you have to give time to practicing the delivery as well as preparing the written sermon.

Extemporaneous Preaching. Preaching without notes or extemporaneous preaching is the type of preaching where the preacher does not take a manuscript or even notes with her into the pulpit. This type of preaching is distinguished from impromptu preaching where the preacher is just preaching "off the cuff." Careful preparation, including often the preparing of a full manuscript, lies behind this method of preaching. It requires not only the necessary preparation of notes or a manuscript but the preparation or "rehearsal" of the sermon before it is preached.

Ilion Jones believes that "free Preaching" has "the possibilities of fulfilling all the essential functions of effective public speaking. Potentially it gives full scope and perfect freedom to the personality of the preacher and provides modern congregations with the conditions of 'listenability,' and the conversational style they desire in public speaking."[81] Many preachers and professors of public speech believe this is the most complete way of speaking. Henry Ward Beecher, F. W. Robertson, Alexander Maclaren, Clovis Chappell, Leslie Weatherhead, John Claypool and others have used this style of preaching. Andrew Blackwood believes that this method is the one most closely identified with biblical and Christian history and thus is the most ideal and natural method of sermon delivery.[82] "Preaching without written aids is a difficult skill to master," Thomas Long observes, "but there is an undeniable authenticity and immediacy when the preacher speaks directly to the listeners with no written 'screen' between them."[83]

Preachers who preach this way have used various methods of preparation. I have used this method for most of my ministry. On occasions I have utilized all of the various methods. But this approach has been my standard practice. After I had used this method for many years, I discovered that Clyde Fant calls this type of preparation "the oral manuscript."[84]

I follow the usual method of preparation mentioned earlier. After I have finished my reading and study, *first, I make a rough draft* putting down thoughts and ideas as they come without a plan and let them flow freely. I jot down and number key phrases and words on a piece of paper and see if there is a pattern. I reflect on the central focus of the text and seek to sort out the sequence of the movements. Sometimes the whole organization seems to fall into place. On other occasions, I have only a vague idea and it is developed slowly and painfully. Sometimes one idea or move carries me to the next; others make me long for where to go. I also think about introduction and conclusion. Sometimes I have those first.

Second, I do my study in various translations and in the commentaries and other books. I make notes for myself as I read and see how the various interpretations compare to what I had sensed. I sometimes check the original languages before I read other translations.

Third, I usually sketch out a final draft that is two to six legal pages long and sometimes more. On these pages are listed the main movements of the sermon and the minor ones beneath with my illustrations and transitions from one movement to the next or to my illustration. I often write out the introduction and the conclusion with five or six sentences each. *Fourth,* If I have time, *I reflect on the sermon as I walk or drive for awhile. Fifth, I then rehearse in my mind* the sermon movements and the transitions, illustrations, etc. on Saturday night. *Sixth*, the next morning *I review them again* before going to church, and after arriving at church and greeting people during Sunday school and dropping by most of the classes, I go to my study and spend at least thirty minutes *rehearsing the sermon again* usually by walking back and forth in my study. I don't memorize it but do memorize the movements, the transitions, the introduction and the way I want to conclude. I have normally been able to deliver the sermon by this method of recall without having notes. On occasions I will take a long quotation written in full.

On special occasions I would write the sermon out in full before I preached it, but most of the time I wrote it out after I preached it or my secretary took it off the tape and I reworked it from her transmission. I furnished my congregation a copy of the sermon the following week.

There are *disadvantages* to doing extemporaneous preaching. (1) It requires for some, certainly for me, more time. There is the preparation for the sermon and then the rehearsal time. (2) There is the risk of forgetting some facet of the sermon. (3) There could be some repetition of words or images. (4) The sermon may not be as polished or as grammatically correct as when written. (5) This method leaves many preachers physically exhausted.

The advantages are numerous. (1) This method allows for more freedom in conversational style, gestures, voice inflections, and facial expressions. (2) The eye contact with the congregation is easier since you are not looking at notes or a manuscript. (3) This style permits greater freshness, enthusiasm, empathy, and charisma. (4) This kind of preaching is easier for congregations to listen to. Lay people say this is their favorite way to listen to preaching. (5) The preacher can read the congregation better and watch their reaction. (6) Some inspiring thoughts may come in the actual delivery of the sermon and she can revise or make changes as she preaches. (7) Although this way may be exhausting, it also can be a very exhilarating experience. (8) The preacher is not totally deterred by external factors like the lights going off and he can't see his notes. (9) The sermon can have more passion and energy.

SOME GENERAL ADVICE

(1) Be yourself. This is the best gift you can give your congregation. Learn from master preachers but don't mimic them. Let the Gospel be mediated through your personality. (2) Use a conversational style of delivery. The more natural you are in your speaking voice the better you will be heard. (3) Avoid a monotone or "stained-glass" voice. Trying to develop a pseudo-preacher tone will not make people listen to you but repel them. (4) Learn to use appropriate gestures and facial expressions. The more natural you are and the more relaxed you become, the better they will be. (5) Try to have natural facial expressions. Don't have a grin on your face the whole time nor be stern-faced the whole time. (6) Dress properly for your congregation. In many churches, the minister wears a robe; in others a suit and tie; in others in contemporary services, the minister will wear simply a casual shirt and slacks. (7) Put force and energy into your delivery. Don't act like the sermon makes no difference to you. It is "the word from the Lord," so act like you believe that in the way you preach. Immerse yourself in the sermon and let it come alive through you. (8) Remember to pray for the guidance of the Holy Spirit in all your preparation and delivery. William Willimon says that "The Holy Spirit may be the most neglected aspect of homiletics today."[85] He does not believe that it is "a sermon until the Holy Spirit enters, speaks, intrudes, and makes it a sermon."[86] And it isn't God's Word for the congregation "unless and until the Holy Spirit descends and enables them to listen."[87]

HELP IN DISCOVERING YOUR STYLE OF DELIVERY

Every preacher needs to discover his or her own style of delivery. Try different methods to see what works best for you. Do not be afraid of trying a new or different way. "The sooner preachers discover their individual styles," John Killinger notes, "the sooner they are able to move into their most productive and useful years of preaching."[88] Listen to criticism from those who want to see you improve. Form a sermon support group in your church or with some ministers in your community, preferably with an ecumenical group. It would be helpful if every minister found a mentor to converse with about his preaching. The mentor could listen to you preach in person or by means of tapes or YouTube. He could offer a critique of your preaching and offer ways to improve. It would also be helpful to take a course or refresher course in speech from a local college. Take advantage of preaching and Bible conferences and continuing education at colleges and seminaries near you. Constantly be working on improving your preaching. Never settle for where you are; further growth is always possible. Remember to be faithful in your sermon preparation and practice a disciplined life of prayer as you seek the guidance of God's Spirit in your preparation and delivery.[89]

REMEMBER THE LISTENERS

The preacher has to remember the people to whom he is preaching. Some congregations may have scholars in their midst but most listeners are ordinary lay persons who desire sermons that are easy to understand yet teach deep truths. Even if highly educated, they do not respond to abstract theological jargon laden with textual critical analysis in the pulpit. They long to hear sermons that are rich with human reality and not filled with literary quotations or allusions. The preacher needs to be aware that most people in the pews have little biblical knowledge. She should not assume that the persons in the pews are familiar with the biblical stories or quotations from the Bible. Lay people also say they often feel that the sermon is not really going anywhere and they wonder what the biblical text has to do with their lives.

Effective preaching will make the listener feel that the preacher is striving to dialogue with his congregation and is conscious of their needs and hopes. Sermon listening groups, worship committees and sermon talk-back sessions can help open the door for lay persons to begin dialoguing with the preacher about her sermons.

Roger Van Harn in his book, *Pew Rights*, reminds the preacher that hearing is central for the congregation and that the sermon is delivered for the congregation. He also asserts that the congregation finishes the sermon and that the test of the value of the sermon lies in what is heard.[90]

The pulpit in the sanctuary of River Road Church, Baptist, where I worship is elevated up high not to glorify the preacher but so the preacher can be seen and heard more easily. The pulpit rest on a chalice-shaped pedestal in the nave of the church and is set out among the congregation to attest to the reality that the preacher is a part of that community of faith. The preacher comes out of the pews to enter the pulpit. The preacher needs to remember that he is linked with the congregation he serves as pastor. During the week he listens to and ministers to the persons in the pews that he will know what to preach on Sunday. Van Harn has reminded us that the sermon is not the possession or product of the preacher (an elite few) but is the responsibility and privilege of the whole church. Continuing he writes:

> When we listen to sermons, we have the right to hear the faith of the church because the sermon comes from the church. The gospel that gave birth to the church is the gospel that is echoed in the church's sermons. When we listen to such sermons, we will hear God's story portrayed, our deepest needs addressed, the burdens imposed upon us by bad religion unloaded, and the testimony of the Apostles resounded.[91]

The preacher needs to reflect each week before she preaches that the congregation has legitimate expectations when they come to listen to sermons and honor those expectations. The preacher who wants others to listen to him has to learn that he too is charged with the responsibility to listen to his congregation before he preaches.

PERSONAL OR GROUP QUESTIONS & REFLECTIONS

1. Name some things you may have experienced that have created a negative atmosphere for preaching on a Sunday for you?
2. What do you think it means to deliver a sermon?
3. Discuss the five methods of sermon delivery. What do you see as the strength or weakness of each?
4. Which method have you found most successful in your preaching? Have you tried any of the others?
5. Have you written a sermon out in a complete manuscript? Was that helpful? Did you take the manuscript with you into the pulpit? Why?
6. Have you tried preaching without notes? How did it go?
7. Have you used a sermon mentor? Was that helpful?
8. How do you judge how well your congregation listens to your sermons?

Selecting Your Display Window:

The Types of Sermons You Preach

I believe that every preacher is not only charged with the responsibility of being biblical but also of being interesting. The sin of dullness has no place in the pulpit, where one is proclaiming the majestic truth of the Gospel of Christ. Shouldn't we strive to preach so people would not merely have to listen but want to listen — no, have to listen? This can be achieved only by investing time and preparation in expounding the biblical and theological truth in an explicable manner. This includes developing verbal images, pictorial phrases, stories that pulsate with life and draw the listener into them as their stories too.

I know a pastor who preached for thirty years in the same church, and his congregation said that no matter what sermon text he selected, he preached the same sermon every week. We don't have to get locked into the same sermonic parlor every week when there are almost endless varieties of windows we can use to guide the congregation into other rooms in the spiritual house. Let's look at some of those possibilities.

Possible Sermon Categories

Lectionary. The first place many ministers will go for their sermon text will be the lectionary. There are four or more Scripture options the preacher can draw from for his sermon. This does not mean, of course, that every sermon from the lectionary has to be the same. Many of the options I will mention can be utilized for the lectionary text. This is the resource many ministers will select first. She can do a deductive or inductive sermon on the text.[92]

A *Topical* or *deductive sermon* is one in which the preacher selects the central biblical idea in the text and focuses the sermon on that theme. Sometimes the preacher of topical sermons first selects his subject, such as "How to Tell Right from Wrong;" "Five Ways to Pray;" or "Following Jesus in Hard Times." Then he looks for a text to match his topic. This was the approach Harry Emerson Fosdick used for many of his sermons. Fosdick based a sermon, "Christians in Spite of Everything" on Philippians 4:21. He lifted the latter part of that text out of Paul's letter and built his sermon with a four point outline around it.[93] Leslie Weatherhead followed a similar pattern in many of his sermons. A sermon for Bible Sunday entitled "Thy Word is Truth" was based on the text John 17:17, "Thy word is Truth," and the text was used as a "launching pad" to discuss the significance of the Bible in our spiritual quest.[94] These sermons obviously do not deal very much with the text but are topic or theme driven and the applications usually are spelled out.

Inductive Sermons. The preacher can use an *inductive approach* toward the text in which the listener is invited to go with the preacher on a quest to discover what the text is saying to the preacher and the listeners. This approach draws on narratives and stories and images rather than a theme or a thesis with a three or more point sermon. Examples of inductive preaching can be seen in Fred Craddock's *Cherry Log Sermons* with his clever use of storytelling and ability to interpret the meaning of the text for the needs of his listeners.[95] This kind of preaching results in what Craddock calls "a nod of recognition," the story the preacher is telling is "my" story too.[96] In this approach the application is not spelled out, but the listener is invited to "overhear" their story in the Bible's story, and the distance between the text and the hearers is bridged, and they become participants in the story itself.[97]

A Narrative Sermon. "A *narrative sermon*" according to Eugene Lowry, "is any sermon in which the arrangement of ideas takes the form of a plot involving a strategic delay of the preacher's meaning."[98] This is a form of inductive preaching which may consist of the telling of a long story, whether biblical or some other form, in which the preacher moves from some conflict which creates a sense of expectancy but may take the hearer to a surprising turn or a reversal of thought. The aim of the sermon is the participation and involvement of the listener. The story or stories function in an indirect mode of communication not direct. The sermons are open-ended, allowing the hearers to reach their own conclusions. The parable of the Good Samaritan, which begins with "a certain man," is told in a fashion that unexpectedly draws the hearers into their own realization that they may indeed be that "certain man" or involved in another unexpected way in the story for today. Many of Frederick Buechner's sermons would fall into this line of preaching.

A good example of narrative or story preaching is the Christmas sermon "Watch, There …," based on Mark 13:32-37 by Charles L. Rice. In story-like fashion, he recounts his experience on a subway in Manhattan where he saw a poster with a child in the snow with a sled and the words on the billboard: "REMEMBER WHEN THIS WAS THE ONLY THING YOU WANTED IN THE WHOLE WORLD?" This question carries him through an inquiry of persons searching and going to who knows where, and of what they are waiting for, and whether their deepest hopes and fears are met in the one who was and is and is to come.[99]

To do narrative preaching well, the preacher has to learn to tell stories well. Just relating stories is not enough. They have to be communicated effectively. The preacher must not neglect the doctrines and biblical truths of our faith which many today do not know. The stories have to help communicate in some fashion the authentic message of the gospel or it will simply be washed up on the shore of well told tales.[100]

Expository Preaching. Some claim to do expository preaching when they merely give a rehash of the biblical text they have just read. Genuine expository preaching requires the preacher to dig deeply into the text through exegesis and sound biblical scholarship and prepare to follow the intention of the text as she lays out her movement through the sermon. The preacher seeks to determine the message in the text and then looks for the proper way to relate the text to the lives of her listeners today. It is not enough to say what the text meant in its day, but the preacher has to guide the hearer in understanding the message the text has for him or her today. Psalm 23, 1 Corinthians 13, and Ephesians 6:10-17, where Paul describes the Christian's armor, all can be powerful expository sermons. In 1 Corinthians 13 the preacher can follow the major moves in the text:

I.   The Contrast of Love vv.1-3

II. The Analysis of Love vv. 4-7

III. The Endurance of Love vv. 8-13.

Through story and word images the preacher follows the movement of the text and seeks to invite the hearers to sense where they enter the story and how the profound message of love relates to their lives.[101]

A textual sermon can be drawn from a single text like the passage from Romans 1:16 "For I am not ashamed of the gospel…" or John 3:16 "For God so loved the world…" or Revelation 3:20 "Behold I stand at the door…" or James 2:17 "So faith by itself, if it has no works, is dead." Again careful exegesis and critical study needs to be done and the relevance for today's listeners has to be shown for the listener to discover her own involvement in the presentation.[102]

Bible Characters. Individual sermons or series of sermon can be preached on various biblical characters. Various series could be preached on the Old Testament patriarchs like Abraham, Moses or Jacob; kings like Saul, David, or Jonathan; prophets like Isaiah, Jeremiah, Amos, Hosea, etc.[103] In the New Testament one could preach on the disciples of Jesus, Paul and his helpers like Timothy, Barnabas, Mark and others. Some have done a series on the women of the Bible[104] or various biblical characters.[105]

Confessional Preaching. John Claypool in his Lyman Beecher Lectures, *The Preaching Event,* lays out his thoughts on this method of preaching. "We will make our greatest impact in preaching," he declares, "when we dare to make available to the woundedness of others what we learn through an honest grappling with our own woundedness."[106] In this sermonic approach the preacher acknowledges her weakness or struggles in certain areas of life and strives to establish a level of trust with the listener who identifies with this woundedness or inefficiency. Thus the preacher shares out of his darkness as well as his light; his struggles as well as his victories; her defeats as well as accomplishments. The preacher declares that he is a "wounded healer," a fellow sufferer, a companion of the sorrowful trail, a sinner saved by grace, still struggling to grow spiritually. The preacher is seeking to call the congregation to identify with her in her Christian walk. Since people usually admire honesty, this approach will appeal to them. People who are hurting can take comfort and guidance in the revelation that the preacher has known that kind of hurting and shares how he has experienced God in that struggle.

In a sermon "The Basis of Hope" with Romans 8:28-39 as a text, Claypool noted that during the last two weeks their life had been filled with the trauma of their eight-year-old daughter being diagnosed with leukemia. His sermon is the struggle with that knowledge and the confession that he had found no answers to the deepest question of this experience. The book he later published after the death of his daughter, which included this sermon, was entitled *Tracks of a Fellow Struggler: How to Handle Grief.*[107] Many were helped by this book, while others found it troublesome. Arthur John Gossip, a Scottish preacher, preached a sermon after the sudden death of his wife, "But When Life Tumbles in, What Then?" with Jeremiah 12:5 as his text.[108] These types of sermons touch a vital nerve in the suffering of others.

The preacher who preaches confessional sermons has to be careful to avoid exhibitionism and not give way to egocentricity. To try to glorify how well you handled doubts, illness, grief, or something else will only serve to alienate you from your congregation not help you identify with them. Most would not want to hear a continual litany of such experiences. The preacher has to be careful that he is offering companionship in their suffering, etc and striving to find God's presence in the midst of it all. This kind of sermon on particular occasions, and done rarely, can be productive.

Experimental Preaching. This type of preaching is an attempt to discover new and creative forms to communicate the sermon more effectively to the contemporary audiences. The preacher is called away from the dreadful seriousness about spiritual things which has so long dominated the sermon. The preacher is challenged to sense the mystery, wonderment and freedom of the spirit and dare to preach in a way that some would see as risky. Some of these sermons are like playlets, letters, parables, mime shows, clown acts, pantomime, Lenten nursery rhymes, music driven, based on movies, and multimedia presentations. The sermons are considered not great sermons but "disposable" ones, religious happenings, if you please.

John Killinger, who introduced this kind of preaching in his preaching classes at Vanderbilt Divinity School in the 1970's, wrote in *Experimental Preaching:* "The only rule is that there are no rules which may not be broken. Real communication is not static and can seldom be accomplished for very long without experimentation and innovation."[109] Examples of these sermons can be found in two books of experimental sermons that Killinger collected.[110]

For many congregations these sermons would be risky, but many contemporary services are good settings for some of these types of sermons. Work with a worship committee and your minister of music and attempt a sermon that might involve youth, children, drama, choirs, and multimedia presentations. Examine Killinger's collections and get some ideas from them. Two books by Thomas Troeger, *Ten Strategies for Preaching in a Multi Media Culture* and *The Parable of Ten Preachers* will also be helpful.[111]

Monologue Sermons. Following closely in the vein of the experimental sermons, monologue sermons can give the preacher an option which is usually fairly well-accepted even in traditional congregations. The minister selects a biblical character and then often dresses in custom for the presentation on Sunday. I have done several of these through the years especially on Children's Sunday. I have dressed like Noah, Jonah, John the Baptist and told their story from their own perspective. I have enjoyed these sermons and so have the congregations. Chris Chapman, pastor at First Baptist Church in Raleigh, North Carolina, has done monologues with good acceptance in that formal church.[112] The monologue requires the preacher to be a bit of an actor and learn his lines well.

Dialogue Sermons. Like the monologue sermon this form also is similar to an experimental sermon. Usually a minister and a fellow minister, or a well-trained lay person, have a dialogue about a religious theme. Sometimes one acts as the unbeliever seeking spiritual guidance or challenging the minister on some theological matter. This leads to an exchange back and forth in the service as they search for an answer. I remember one college assembly where the preacher was speaking about how Christians should be followers of Jesus and go wherever he leads. In the midst of the preacher saying this, a young man stood up in the balcony and interrupted the sermon. "You Christians don't mean a word of that. You will not really go anywhere Jesus leads." After a moment of stunned silence, the minister began to address the young man's question and the dialogue began. It was attention getting and the dialogue was effective and helpful in trying to discern what the Christian means by saying she will follow Jesus anywhere. This type of sermon takes study and careful planning and staging.

Communion and Baptismal Sermons. Special sermons can be planned for communion and baptismal services focusing on the meaning of the Lord's Supper and the significance of baptism in the lives of those bring baptized, their family and the church.

Doctrinal Sermons. Most of the members either have almost no knowledge of what our basic Christian beliefs are or have only a vague acquaintance with them. These types of sermons, which are teaching sermons, can focus on the great doctrines of our faith like sin, salvation, the cross, the resurrection of Jesus, religious experience, grace, faith, the Church, eternal life. I have often done a series of sermons on various aspects of our beliefs, such as a series on "Who Is Jesus Christ?" "What's Beyond Death? Or I have approached it through a study of our Baptist heritage and beliefs. You could do a similar thing in your denomination.[113]

Ethical Sermons. Our church members like all people struggle every day with ethical decision making. The church needs to offer some direction in these matters. Our standard is Christ and we seek to follow his life and teachings in the way we live and think. Again I often preach series of sermons related to some ethical theme like "How to live like a Christian in Today's Society." I have preached sermons like "Living at Peace with the Environment" with Scriptures Romans 8:19-20 and Revelation 21:1, 22:1-2; "Waging Peace," Matthew 5:9; and sermons on "The Playboy Philosophy" and "Situation Ethics."

Pastoral Sermons. Sermons that address the human struggles of our congregation are met with open ears and arms. To know that that the preacher in the pulpit is conscious of their needs engages their attention and response. Calvin Miller introduces the first chapter in his book, *The Empowered Communicator*, with an enthralling letter he penned as though it was written by "the Audience" to whom we preach. The letter notes that the preacher's speech will never reach his ears until the preacher sees the person in the audience as she really is. Continuing he writes:

> I am loneliness waiting for a friend.
> I am weeping in want of laughter.
> I am a sigh in search of consolation.
> I am a wound in search of compress.[114]

"If you want to unlock my attention," he concludes, "you have but to convince me you want to be my friend. When you make me feel like I am the only person in this vast audience, I will give you what I have given to very few: the unbroken focus of my mind."[115] Anger, loneliness, depression, anxiety, suffering, grief, are all a part of our daily pilgrimage and we long for assurance, support and spiritual guidance. I have often preached various series of sermons to speak to these needs like "Facing Grief and Death," "Handling the Struggles of Living," and "Where Is God When I Hurt?" Often I begin with the need and then search for a text that addresses that need.[116]

Funeral and Wedding Sermons. I believe funeral sermons should be brief, about ten or twelve minutes long, and should seek to offer comfort to the family and assurance of our Christian belief in life after death. They are not evangelistic services and should not be turned in that direction. That usually is offensive to the family. Unbelievers can overhear the Gospel when it is proclaimed, and that is sufficient, I believe. Thomas Long's book, *Accompany Them with Singing: The Christian Funeral,* can offer significant help to the pastor in this area.[117]

My wedding "sermonet" is usually only a few minutes in length, two or three minutes long, and usually focuses on the significance of Christian marriage, their love for each other, the new family they are establishing, and the importance of the vows they are exchanging before God and the gathered church.

Other types of sermon windows could include a focus on evangelism, missions, Children or Youth Sundays, Senior Adult Sundays, special events such as church anniversaries or celebrations or many others.

These are only a few of the display windows the preacher might select to present his sermon. A variety of windows may beckon more of those who want to listen. Whatever way he selects, the goal is to enable the listener to see through that particular window the proclamation of the good news of the Gospel. It is a desire to accomplish more than getting someone to see but to hear and respond in some way to the power of the proclaimed word. The preacher always preaches with the timidity of knowing that she is speaking a word on "behalf of God,' and surely this will always cause one to weigh carefully what and how that word is proclaimed.

PERSONAL OR GROUP QUESTIONS & REFLECTIONS

1. Have you been able to expand your preaching source beyond
    the lectionary?
2. What other ways of preaching have been helpful to you in
    your preaching?
3. How has your congregation responded to them?
4. How have you maintained a vital connection with the biblical
    text in your sermon no matter what format you used? Do you
    think that is really important?
5. What type of sermon have you preached, like a confessional
    or experimental kind, and what was the response from your
    congregation?
6. Do you think there is a need to preach doctrinal and ethical
    sermons today? How would you undertake that approach, if
    you believe there is a need?
7. Describe what your funeral and wedding sermons are like?

FEELING AND HEARING THE SERMON:

ADDRESSING THE INTUITION AS WELL AS THE INTELLECT

When I first began to teach preaching at the Southern Baptist Theological Seminary in Louisville, Kentucky, one of the books that deeply influenced me and I used as a text, along with several others, in my basic preaching class, was *The Recovery of Preaching* by Henry Mitchell. The book, published in 1977, was his 1974 Lyman Beecher Lectures given at Yale Divinity School. I found his message to be of vital importance for all my ministerial students. I believe that his insights are still important for preachers today, and I want to share some of them and note why I think they are so significant today.

PREACH TO THE WHOLE PERSON

First, preaching has to *address the whole person* and not just the intellectual side. Too much of preaching is directed to changing the mind of the hearer and ignores the total person. Much of our thinking and living is compartmentalized and fragmented. Over fifty years ago that hurricane of a preacher, Carlyle Marney, asked the question, "Who sees the whole man?"

The doctor sees the organ or tissue of his specialty. The dentist sees mostly a mouth. The lawyer sees a litigant. The realtor sees only a prospect and may not know the tragedy that makes the seller sell. The mechanic, under the car, sees his client feet-to-knees at best. The undertaker does not see the whole man, he sees what is left of the whole man. The newsman sees only some extraordinary aspect that makes a man into news. The salesman looks for the prospects, and so does the professional pastor. The white provincial holy man looks only for the white, the provincial, and the pious. Who sees the whole man?[118]

Who is this I/me, you/they, he/she person that the preacher speaks to every week? It is man and woman, adult and child, young and old, rested and tired, alert and sleepy, happy and sad, believing and unbelieving, ill and healthy, interested and uninterested. Persons from many walks of life and various perspectives sit before the preacher. Some with anticipation; others bored and longing to be elsewhere are in the congregation.

He /she is body and soul, flesh and spirit, mind and matter, intellect and feeling, rational and intuitive. To reach these persons the preacher has to address the whole person — the unconscious self, the intuitive self, the existential self, the emotional self, the "gut" level self, as well as the rational self. The preacher, in spite of society's isolationist's view of life, has to see man and woman, adult and child in their "total" self, if his message is to reach them. Mitchell challenges the preacher to speak to the unconscious and subconscious level of her listeners, to address the cultural symbols that may be buried deeply in their subconscious and seek to retrieve and access them. "Preaching that makes meaningful impact on lives," Mitchell asserts, "has to reach persons at gut level, and it is at this level of communally stored wisdom and culture affinity that such access to living souls is gained."[119]

Preaching has to address what Mitchell calls "the transconscious" level within persons. This is that inner dimension where may be buried the spiritual and emotional symbols and subconscious feelings we have long ignored or forgotten. Mitchell recounts the story of a Black prostitute, who had divorced herself from the church and its teachings. However, when she was in labor, regardless of her use of profanity or dope, she cleaned up her speech and cried out, "O Lord, have mercy!" She reached back to the inner culture out of which she had come.[120] The Scottish theologian, John Baillie, affirmed this belief with his interpretation of religious knowledge with the insight that some people might deny God with the "top of their mind" but still believe in God in the "bottom of their heart."[121] Consequently, the preacher strives to preach to the bottom of the heart as well as to the top of the mind to reach the deepest existential feelings or needs of the listeners.

GIVE AN EYE WITNESS ACCOUNT

Second, the preacher has to give *an eye witness perspective* on what she is proclaiming. The story the preacher is proclaiming has to be internalized and preached not from some distance but from one who has lived with the experience and seeks to recreate the action and communicate the experience. For example, the preacher doesn't just talk about grace and conversion in the abstract but in concrete personal experience. "Here's how my life was changed one day by God's interrupting power! I was going my usual way in my work, when suddenly …" And you share your story. In a moving account of his conversion, a Black preacher said: "I can tell you the day and the hour when my dungeon shook and my chains fell off. I looked at my hands, and my hands looked new. I looked at my feet, and they did too."[122]

In some way the preacher must give an eye witness account and not merely a second-hand explanation of an experience. Your spiritual experience and theology have been internalized and now you broadcast the reality of that experience in your preaching. Like John, the elder, in the *Book of Revelation*, you proclaim: "I, John, down on the Isle of Patmos reveal to you …" A student in one of my preaching classes preached a sermon on fasting. After he finished preaching the sermon and we were critiquing him, I asked him if he had ever fasted. He said he had. I then asked, "Why did you not tell us that? It would have made your sermon believable." Preaching is not delivering an essay on some theme. The preacher has to be involved in the sermon, not divorced from it, for it to be a meaningful experience for the hearers.

Sometimes when an athlete is not doing well in his sport, we may say, "He was just not into his game today." The same can be said of preachers on a particular Sunday. "She was just not into her sermon today!" The sermon has to be internalized and not preached from a distance from the text. It has to be a genuine experience the preacher has encountered so as to recreate the action and communicate that experience to others. This perspective challenges "distance" in preaching and calls the preacher to be intimate and personal and not act like a disinterested party. This affirms the humanness of preaching and the involvement of the preacher in the sermon itself. Allowing distance between the preacher and the message he is proclaiming would be finally fatal. A preacher, of course, cannot declare an experience she has not had. But shouldn't a preacher be like the Apostle Paul, who said: "Woe to me if I do not proclaim the gospel!" (1 Cor. 9:16). Our religious experience longs to be preached, no — must be preached. Get inside the biblical story and learn to tell it, Mitchell encourages, from your own frame of reference and perspective. It will come more alive for the listeners as they visualize what the preacher has experienced.[123]

THE INVOLVEMENT OF THE PREACHER WITH THE SERMON

The congregation will affirm that the message is worth listening to if they believe the one proclaiming the sermon is worth listening to. The listeners will not trust the message if they cannot trust the teller of the message. I remember hearing a preacher say that, although he was still preaching because he needed the money, he no longer believed what he preached. That kind of distance from our message isn't only dishonest; it's fatal to the preacher's ability to communicate his message. If we no longer believe the gospel message, how can we expect others to believe it?

The preacher should first be addressed by the message she proclaims herself. If one finger points to the listeners as we preach, are not four other fingers directed toward us? How can a preacher possibly preach without being altered by the message he proclaims?

Only an Elmer Gantry or a huckster can preach that way, not an authentic man or woman of God. If there is no real "I" in our preaching, I do not believe we can elicit others to respond. The preacher is inescapably involved with the sermon she preaches and is never exempt from its judgment, hope, promise, demand or assurance.

PAINT PICTURES TO COMMUNICATE

To preach transconciously the preacher has to learn to translate the message into a story or picture. Mitchell believes that if the preacher cannot tell the gospel message in "moving and graphic art and symbol — word pictures and narrations," he should not preach it. He reminds us that people don't think logically, they think analogically. Painted pictures and stories presented in abundant, realistic and striking detail give the listeners spiritual "handles" they can put their thought around and take the message with them.[124] Mitchell reminds us that the best of Black preaching has been communicated by art and not by argument. This does not mean that it is not logical, he notes, but is logical on levels other than just rational ones. It addresses the intuition, feelings, emotions, sensitivities, subtle mentality and the unconscious as well as the intelligence and obvious mentality.[125]

SPEAK TO HUMAN NEEDS

These dramatic images in preaching will address the deepest needs of the listeners and will draw them into the sermon as they long for a message of encouragement, guidance, reassurance, hope, and support. This method makes the Bible live again as the listeners are drawn into the Bible stories as their stories and the biblical message as their message. When the listeners feel that the preacher has sat where they sit, they will more readily respond to the message she preaches. If she knows my needs and has "scratched where I itch," then I will take notice and listen.[126] When the preacher preaches pastoral sermons, situational sermons or sermons that speak to human needs, the listeners will be able to see how the biblical text applies directly to their lives. This is an important dimension of preaching which too many pastors ignore at their peril. If a pastor will listen to her congregation for at least twenty hours in a week and share in their struggles, grief, burdens, happiness and joys during this time, she will have a right to preach to them for twenty minutes on Sunday morning and they will listen better.

PREACHING AS CELEBRATION

Preaching without celebration, according to Mitchell, is really a denial of the good news. "Preaching with celebration," Mitchell declares, "enhances the transconscious retention and the true understanding and application of the gospel."[127] If the gospel message is preached joyfully and received in a joyful way, it will be likely unforgettable. Those who express gratitude for the good news will draw others into the community of faith. The preacher should focus on the great themes of the faith that have celebration at their center. Again the preacher must be involved in the sermon. Celebration is more caught than taught. As the preacher is in the "telling," the listeners will catch the celebration and be drawn into the joyous story as their story as well.[128]

The preacher who makes preaching dull and boring needs to go back to his study and labor to be interesting. He needs to discover the "wonder" of the word which James Howell writes about. Howell acknowledges that we all fail at times in trying to preach the word and that assures our sense of humility. But we keep on striving to find the words to proclaim to fulfill the wonder of the word. "We borrow, beg, steal words, trying them on for size, shaking our heads, trying again," he observes. "The preacher's words tiptoe along a treacherous line, where words provoke, dare, strain, wait, and try once more."[129] We need to return again and again to that place where we can perfect our preaching, knowing always that we want to offer God our best gifts. In his Lyman Beecher Lectures, *What's Good about This News?* David Bartlett notes that the one thing that students remember about his lectures is that he told them that "preaching is always good news." "It is not the repetition of tired formulas ... Preaching is a lively word."[130] Let's never forget that!

FEELING IN PREACHING

I was talking with a friend recently about a certain preacher we both had heard preach. We both stated that something was missing from his sermon the last time we heard him preach. He had been exciting to listen to before, but this time he was not into the sermon at all. He lacked energy, force, enthusiasm, or feeling. An effective sermon will not be one where the preacher appears detached or distant from the message she is preaching. Personal involvement is essential. The preacher's "excitement" about the message she is preaching will ignite fire in her listeners. I believe that only fire kindles fire. If the preacher does not "feel" the message, he will not be able to get his listeners to feel it. Whatever one wants to call it, force, energy, passion, feeling or enthusiasm, without it a preacher is ineffective no matter how good what he has on a piece of paper in front of him is.

Without minimizing the role of intellect, volition or will in a preacher's sermon, Fred Craddock affirms the importance of emotion in the delivery of a sermon. "Some desire to have more passion for the pulpit. I hear a frequent lament of an absence of passion in the pulpit and I don't know why," Craddock observes. "No stirring of the heart and mind on the part of the minister. And your listener senses the absence of emotional engagement as you don't believe your own sermon, or you don't think it is important. That is the way it is telegraphed to the listener."[131] Craddock believes that there is an "under-appreciation for emotion" in preaching and he urges the preacher to learn to preach "once more with feeling."[132] Let us pray the prayer of George Matheson.

> Reveal to me, O Lord, that fire which burns and yet does not consume — the fire of love! My life will be consumed

without the burning of that fire. It is want of enthusiasm that kills me, wears me away. My soul dies through lack of burning. I never really live unless I catch fire … I am never so weary as when I am aimless, never so fatigued as when I have nothing to do. Set fire to my heart, O Lord. Kindle me into the love of humanity! Inflame me with the passion to make my brother glad … Lay on my heart the burden of the bondsman, the troubles of the toiler, the weights of the weary. Help me to live in the experience of human struggle.[133]

Set me on fire, O Lord, when I preach!

PERSONAL OR GROUP QUESTIONS & REFLECTIONS

1. How can the preacher learn to preach to the transconscious level of his listeners?
2. Can this be done without playing on the emotions of your listeners?
3. In what ways can the preacher "sit" where his people are? What kind of pastoral needs might she encounter and how can one preach to them?
4. What role do stories play in helping the hearer to grasp the sermon's meaning? How do you try to build pictorial images and illustrations into your sermons?
5. What do you believe it means to talk about a preacher having force in his preaching? Can this passion be learned?

SELECTED PREACHING RESOURCES

Bartlett, David L. *Between the Bible and the Church: New Methods for Biblical Preaching* (Nashville: Abingdon Press, 1999).

_____. *What's Good about This News?* (Louisville: Westminster John Knox Press, 2003).

Brosend, William. *The Preaching of Jesus: Gospel Proclamation Then and Now* (Louisville: Westminster John Knox Press, 2010).

Claypool, John, *The Preaching Event* (Waco, TX: Word Books, Inc., 1988).

Cornwall, Robert D. *Unfettered Spirit: Spiritual Gifts for the New Great Awakening* (Gonzalez, FL: Energion Publications, 2013).

Cox, James W. *Preaching: A Comprehensive Approach to the Design and Delivery of Sermons* (San Francisco: Harper & Row Publishers, 1985).

Craddock, Fred B. *As One Without Authority,* revised edition (St Louis, Missouri: Chalice Press, 2001).

_____. *Craddock on the Craft of Preaching,* edited by Lee Sparks & Kathryn Hayes Sparks (St. Louis, Missouri: Chalice Press, 2011).

_____. *Overhearing the Gospel,* revised and expanded (St. Louis, Missouri: Chalice Press, 2002).

_____. *Preaching* (Nashville: Abingdon Press, 1985).

Dupier, Jr., Charles Mayer, *The Artful Science of Preaching* (Cleveland, TN: Parson's Porch Books, 2010).

Fasol, Al. *A Complete Guide to Sermon Delivery* (Nashville: Broadman Press, 1996).

Howell, James. *The Beauty of the Word: The Challenge and Wonder of Preaching* (Louisville: Westminster John Knox Press, 2011).

Jacks, G. Robert, *Getting the Word Across: Speech Communication for Pastors and Lay Leaders* (Grand Rapids: William B. Eerdmans Publishing Co., 1995).

Killinger, John. editor, *Experimental Preaching* (Nashville: Abingdon Press, 1973).

_____. *Fundamentals of Preaching*, revised edition (Minneapolis: Fortress Press, 1996).

_____. editor, *The 11 O'clock News & Other Experimental Sermons* (Nashville: Abingdon press, 1975).

Lathrop, Gordon W. *The Pastor: A Spirituality* (Minneapolis: Fortress Press, 2006).

Long, Thomas G. *Accompany Them with Singing: The Christian Funeral* (Louisville: Westminster John Knox Press, 2009).

_____. *The Witness of Preaching*, second edition (Louisville: Westminster John Knox Press, 2005).

Lowry, Eugene L. *The Homiletical Beat: Why All Sermons Are Narrative* (Nashville: Abingdon Press, 2012).

_____. *The Homiletical Plot* (Atlanta: John Knox Press, 1975).

Lundblad, Barbara K. *Marking Time: Preaching Biblical Stories in Present Tense* (Nashville: Abingdon Press, 2007).

Miller, Calvin. *The Empowered Communicator* (Nashville: Broadman & Holman Publishers, 1994).

Mitchell, Henry H. *Celebration and Experience in Preaching* (Nashville: Abingdon Press, 1990).

_____. *The Recovery of Preaching* (San Francisco: Harper & Row, 1977).

Meyers, E. B., *Expository Preaching: Plan and Methods* (Grand Rapids: Baker Books, 1974).

Plantinga, Jr., Cornelius. *Reading for Preaching: The Preacher in Conversation with Storytellers, Biographers, Poets, and Journalists* (Grand Rapids, Michigan: William B. Eerdmans, Publishing Co., 2013).

Reid, Robert Stephen and Lucy Lind Hogan, *The Six Deadly Sins of Preaching: Becoming Responsible for the Faith We Proclaim* (Nashville: Abingdon Press, 2012).

Shepherd, J. Barrie. *Whatever Happened to Delight? Preaching the Gospel in Poetry and Parables* (Louisville: Westminster John Knox Press, 2006).

Steimle, Edmund A, Morris J. Niedenthal and Charles L. Rice, *Preaching the Story* (Philadelphia: Fortress Press, 1980).

Taylor, Barbara Brown, *The Preaching Life* (Cambridge: Cowley Publications, 1993).

_____. *When God Is Silent* (Cambridge: Cowley Publications, 1998).

Tisdale, Leonora Tubbs. *Preaching as Local Theology and Folk Art* (Philadelphia: Fortress Press, 1997).

Tuck, William Powell. *A Pastor Preaching: Toward a Theology of the Proclaimed Word* (Macon. GA: Nurturing Faith, 2012).

Van Harn, Roger E., *Pew Rights* (Grand Rapids, Michigan: William B. Eerdmans Publishing Co., 1992).

William H. Willimon, *Undone by Easter: Keeping Preaching Fresh* (Nashville: Abingdon Press, 2009).

COMMENTARIES IN SERIES

Individual commentaries by selected authors are the best way to build your library.

Barclay, William. *The Daily Study Bible Series,* 18 volumes, Westminster Press (Older but still helpful).

Gibson, John C. L. *The Daily Study Bible Series for The Old Testament,* Westminster Press. Each volume is written by a different writer, 24 volumes.

May, James L. series editor, *Interpretation: A Bible Commentary for Teaching and Training,* John Knox Press. Each volume is written by a different writer, 31 volumes.

Smyth & Helwys Bible Commentaries (Macon, Georgia: Smyth & Helwys Publishers). Each commentary is written by a different writer, 28 volumes.

The New Interpreter's Bible (Nashville: Abingdon Press), 12 volumes. Each volume is written by a different writer.

Wright, N. T., *New Testament for Everyone* series (Louisville: Westminster John Knox Press, 2011).

PREACHING SERIES

Fant, Jr., Clyde E. and William M. Pinson, editors, *20 Centuries of Great Preaching* (Waco, TX: Word Books Publisher, 1971) 13 volumes.

Klingsporn, Gary W., general editor, *The Library of Distinctive Sermons* (Sisters, Oregon: Questar Publisher, 1996-forward), 9 volumes.

PREACHING ENCYCLOPEDIAS

Willimon, William H. and Richard Lischer, editors, *Concise Encyclopedia of Preaching* (Louisville: Westminster John Knox Press, 1995).

Wilson, Paul Scott, *The New Interpreters' Handbook of Preaching* (Nashville: Abingdon Press, 2008).

LECTIONARY HELPS

Books:

Allen, Ronald J. and Clark M. Williamson, *Preaching the Gospels Without Blaming the Jews: A Lectionary Commentary* (Louisville: Westminster John Knox Press, 2004).

_____ *Preaching the Letters Without Dismissing the Law: A Lectionary Commentary* (Louisville: Westminster John Knox Press, 2006).

_____ *Preaching the Old Testament: A Lectionary Commentary* (Louisville: Westminster John Knox Press, 2007).

Bartlett, David L. and Barbara Brown Taylor, *Feasting on the Word: Preaching the Revised Common Lectionary* (Louisville: Westminster John Knox Press, 2010—forward) (Volumes I & II published in 2010 and additional volumes being published)

Fuller, Reginald Horace and David Westberg, *Preaching the Lectionary*, third edition (Collegeville, Minnesota: Liturgical Press, 2006).

Various denominations issue their own lectionary like the *Lutheran Service Book, Episcopal- Daily Office Reading, Catholic—Lectionary-Sunday Mass (Pulpit)*

Internet Resources:

(There are many denominational resources. Among the many others, I recommend the following.)

Textweek.com
Workingpreacher.org
Vanderbilt lectionary
Lectionary preaching resources
Open Source Lectionary.com/tools for preachers
CSS Publishing
www.nurturingfaith.net/blog.

ENDNOTES

1   Dietrich Bonhoeffer, *God Is on the Cross* (Louisville: Westminster John Knox Press, 2012), 8.

2   Powhatan W. James, *George W. Truett: A Biography* (New York: The Macmillan Company, 1940), 45f.

3   Frederick Buechner, *The Alphabet of Grace* (New York: The Seabury Press, 1977), 109-110.

4   Fred Brenning Craddock, *Reflections on My Call to Preach* ((St. Louis, Missouri: Chalice Press, 2009), 113.

5   William Powell Tuck, *Modern Shapers of Baptist Thought in America* (Richmond, Virginia: Center for Baptist Heritage & Studies, 2012), 394.

6   Gardner C. Taylor, "Why I Believe There Is a God," in *Why I Believe There Is a God*, edited by Howard Thurman (Chicago: Johnson Publishing Co., 1965), 86.

7   Henlee Hulix Barnette, *A Pilgrimage of Faith* (Macon, Georgia: Macon University Press, 2004), 28-31.

8   Barbara Brown Taylor, *Leaving Church: A Memoir of Faith* (San Francisco: Harper Collins, 2006), 35.

9   Paul Tournier, *The Meaning of Gifts* (Richmond, Virginia: John Knox Press, 1963), 47.

10   Robert D. Cornwall, Unfettered Spirit: Spiritual Gifts for the New Great Awakening (Gonzalez, FL: Energion Publications, 2013), 37.

11   Loren Eiseley, *The Unexpected Universe* (New York: Harcourt, Brace & World, Inc., 1969), 31.

12   W. MacNeile Dixon, *The Human Situation* (New York: Longmans, Green, 1937). 429. See also my book, *Through the Eyes of a Child* (New York: Writers Club Press, 2003), especially 1-47.

13   David L. Bartlett, *What's Good about This News?* (Louisville: Westminster John Knox Press, 2003), 2.

14   Ibid, 10.

15   Robert Stephen Reid and Lucy Lind Hogan, *The Six Deadly Sins of Preaching: Becoming Responsible for the Faith We Proclaim* (Nashville: Abingdon Press, 2012), 103.

16   See the "Preaching Resources" for further suggestions.

17   See a new work by Scott M. Gibson, *Preaching with a Plan* (Grand Rapids, Michigan: Baker Books, 2012).

18   Several works by the following persons may be helpful: E. Glen Hinson, *A Serious Call to a Contemplative Lifestyle* (Macon, GA: Smyth & Helwys, 1993), *Spirituality in Ecumenical Perspective* (Louisville: Westminster John Knox Press, 1993*), Spiritual Preparation for Christian Leadership* (Nashville: The Upper Room, 2000); Henri J. M. Nouwen, *Can You Drink This Cup?* (Notre Dame, Indiana: Ave Maria Press, 1996), *Show Me the Way: Daily Lenten Readings* (New York: Crossroad Book, 2011); Richard J. Foster, *Celebration of Discipline: The Path to Spiritual Growth* (San Francisco: Harper & Row, 1988); Kent Ira Groff, *Honest to God Prayer: Spirituality as Awareness, Empowerment, Relinquishment and Paradox* (Woodstock, Vermont: Skylight Paths Publisher, 2013); Joyce Rupp, *The Cup of Life: A Guide for Spiritual Growth* (Notre Dame, Indiana: Ave Maria Press, 1998).

19   Ronald Klug, *How to Keep a Spiritual Journal* (Minneapolis: Augsburg Press, 1993), Francis Loftis Carroll, *The Christian Diary: A Personal Journal for Bible Study, Prayer, and Spiritual Growth* (Englewood Cliffs, New Jersey: Prentice-Hall, Inc., 1984).

20   Harry Emerson Fosdick, *Riverside Sermons* (New York: Harper & Brothers, 1958), 275ff.

21   Leonard Griffith, *God's Time and Ours* (New York: Abingdon Press, 1964), 109ff.

22   John Killinger, *Christmas Is Spoken Here* (Nashville: Broadman Press, 1989), 76ff.

23   William Powell Tuck, *Getting Past the Pain: Making Sense of Life's Darkness* (Macon, GA: Smyth & Helwys Publishing Co., 1997) and *Facing Life's Ups and Downs* (Macon, GA: Smyth & Helwys, 2010).

24   Leander E. Keck, *The Bible in the Pulpit* (Nashville: Abingdon Press, 1978), 115.

25   Ibid.

26   William Powell Tuck, *A Pastor Preaching: Toward a Theology of the Proclaimed Word* (Macon, GA: Nurturing Faith, Inc., 2012), 47ff.

27   See the following books for additional suggestions on examining the text: James Cox, *Preaching: A Comprehensive Approach to the Design and Delivery of Sermons* (San Francisco: Harper & Row, 1985), 73-76; Fred B. Craddock, *Preaching* (Nashville: Abingdon Press, 1985), 113-124; Thomas G. Long, *The Witness of Preaching,* Second Edition, (Louisville: Westminster John Knox Press, 2005), 81-96.

28   Craddock, *Preaching*, 122-123.

29   Cox, *Preaching*, 76.

30   Long, *The Witness of Preaching*, 97.

31   James C. Howell, *The Beauty of the Word* (Louisville: Westminster, John Knox Press, 2011), 17.

32   J. H. Jowett, *The Preacher: His Life and Work* (New York: Abingdon Press, 1912), 133.

33   See, for example, this argument in Thomas G. Long, *The Witness of Preaching* (Louisville: Westminster John Knox Press, 2005), 100-105.; and the pioneering work by Fred B. Craddock, *As One Without Authority: Essays on Inductive Preaching* (Enid, Oklahoma: The Phillips University Press, 1971).

34   Henri J. M. Nouwen, *The Return of the Prodigal Son: A Study of Homecoming* (New York: Doubleday, 1994), 121.

35   John Killinger, *Fundamentals of Preaching* (Minneapolis: Fortress Press, 1996), 92.

36   Ibid, 94.

37   James W. Cox, *Preaching: A Comprehensive Approach to the Design and Delivery of Sermons* (San Francisco: Harper & Row, 1985), 168.

38   Thomas G. Long, *The Witness of Preaching*, second edition (Louisville: Westminster John Knox Press, 2005), 186.

39   Ibid, 181.

40   Kelly Miller Smith, "The Search," in William Powell Tuck, editor, *The Struggle for Meaning* (Valley Forge, PA: Judson Press, 1977), 11.

41   Peter J. Gomes, *Sermons: Biblical Wisdom for Daily Living* (New York: William Morrow and Inc., 1998), 154.

42   Robert J. McCracken, *The Making of the Sermon* (New York: Harper and Brothers, nd), 92.

43   Harry Emerson Fosdick, *Living Under Tension* (New York: Harper & Brothers, 1941), 222.

44   William Powell Tuck, *The Last Words from the Cross* (Gonzalez, FL: Energion Publications, 2013), 65.

45   Robert J. McCracken, *Questions People Ask* (New York: Harper & Brothers, 1951).

46   Fred B Craddock, *The Cherry Log Sermons* (Louisville: Westminster John Knox Press, 2001) and Fred B. Craddock, *The Collected Sermons of Fred B. Craddock* (Louisville: Westminster John Knox Press, 2011).

47   John Killinger, *Christmas Is Spoken Here* (Nashville: Broadman Press, 1989), 11.

48   Herbert H. Farmer, *The Servant of the Word* (New York: Charles Scribner's Sons, 1942), 65.

49   Ernest Campbell, *Locked in a Room with Open Doors* (Waco, Texas: Word Books, 1974), 19.

50   Barbara Brown Taylor, *Gospel Medicine* (Cambridge: Cowley Publications, 1995), 23.

51   William H. Willimon, *The Collected Sermons of William H. Willimon* (Louisville: Westminster John Knox Press, 2010), 97.

52   Leslie Weatherhead, "The Modern Christian and Sunday" in *Best Sermons*, Volume VIII, edited by G. Paul Butler (New York: D. Van Nostrand Co., Inc., 1962), 311.

53   William Sloane Coffin, *The Collected Sermons of William Sloane Coffin*, Volume 2 (Louisville: Westminster John Knox Press, 2008), 444.

54   Halford E. Luccock, *In the Minister's Workshop* (New York: Abingdon-Cokesbury Press, 1944), 121.

55   See for example Andrew W. Blackwood, *The Preparation of Sermons* (New York: Abingdon-Cokesbury, 1948), 136ff; Ilion T. Jones, *Principles and Practices of Preaching* (New York: Abingdon Press, 1956), 103ff; George E. Sweazey, *Preaching the Good News* ((Englewood Cliffs, New Jersey: Prentice-Hall, 1976), 82ff.

56   David Buttrick, *Homiletic: Moves and Structures* (Philadelphia: Fortress Press, 1987), 24.

57   Among many writings, see, for example, Fred Craddock, *As One Without Authority* and *Overhearing the Gospel* (Nashville: Abingdon Press, 1978); Eugene L. Lowry, *The Homiletical Plot: The Sermon as Narrative* (Atlanta: John Knox Press, 1980); Paul Scott Wilson, *The Four Pages of the Sermon: A Guide to Biblical Preaching* (Nashville: Abingdon Press, 1999); and Thomas G. Long, *The Witness of Preaching*, second edition (Louisville: Westminster John Knox Press, 2005).

58   A. Leonard Griffith, *What Is a Christian?* (New York: Abingdon Press, 1961), 133-141.

59   Long, *The Witness of Preaching*, 125.

60   Fred B. Craddock, *As One Without Authority* (Enid, Oklahoma: The Philips University Press, 1971), 51ff.

61   Fred B. Craddock, *Craddock on the Craft of Preaching*, edited by Lee Sparks & Kathryn Hayes Sparks (St. Louis, Missouri: Chalice Press, 2011), 193.

62   Ibid. 41.

63   Karl Barth, *Deliverance to the Captives* (New York: Harper and Row Publishers, 1961), 35ff.

64   This was published in William Powell Tuck, *Authentic Evangelism: Sharing the Good News with Sense and Sensitivity* (Valley Forge: Judson Press, 2002), 112-121.

65   Frederick W. Robertson, *Sermons Preached at Brighton* (New York: Harper & Brothers, n d), 426-436.

66   James S. Stewart, *The Strong Name* (New York: Charles Scribner's Sons, 1941), 90-101.

67   Thomas G. Long, *The Witness of Preaching*, second edition (Louisville: Westminster John Knox Press, 2005). 200-220.

68   See, for example, Archibald M. Hunter, *Interpreting the Parables*, (Philadelphia: Westminster Press, 1960), 11.

69   T. W. Manson, *The Teachings of Jesus* (Cambridge: University Press, 1935), 73.

70   Kenneth E. Bailey, *Through Peasant Eyes* (Grand Rapids, Michigan: William B. Eerdmans Publishing Company, 1980), xi.

71   Charles L. Rice, *The Embodied Word: Preaching as Art and Liturgy* (Minneapolis: Fortress Press, 1991), 98.

72   W. MacNeile Dixon, *The Human Situation* (New York: Longmans, Green & Co., n d), 65.

73   Ibid, 66.

74   Henry H. Mitchell, *The Recovery of Preaching* (San Francisco: Harper & Row, 1977), 47.

75   Ibid, 45.

76   Barbara Brown Taylor, *The Preaching Life* (Cambridge: Cowley Publications, 1993), 79.

77   Long, *The Witness of Preaching*, 204-220.

78   William Powell Tuck, *Love as a Way of Living* (Macon, GA: Smyth & Helwys, 2008), 89-90.

79   Charles Mayer Dupier, Jr., *The Artful Science of Preaching* (Cleveland, TN: Parson's Porch Books, 2010), 17.

80   Roger Van Harn, *Pew Rights: For People Who Listen to Sermons* (Grand Rapids, Michigan: William B. Eerdmans Publishing Co., 1992), 79.

81   Ilion T. Jones, *Principles and Practice of Preaching* (New York: Abingdon Press, 1956), 202.

82   Andrew W. Blackwood, *The Preparation of Sermons* (New York: Abingdon-Cokesbury, 1948), 194-196. See also John A. Broadus *On the Preparation and Delivery of Sermons*, new and revised edition by Jesse Burton Weatherspoon (Nashville: Broadman Press, 1944), 325ff.

83   Thomas G. Long, *The Witness of Preaching*, second edition (Louisville: Westminster John Knox Press, 2005), 227.

84   Clyde E. Fant, *Preaching for Today* (New York: Harper & Row, 1975), 118ff.

85   William H. Willimon, *Undone by Easter: Keeping Preaching Fresh* (Nashville: Abingdon, 2009), 89.

86   *Ibid.*

87   *Ibid*, 25.

88   John Killinger, *Fundamentals of Preaching*, second edition (Minneapolis: Fortress Press, 1996), 148.

89   Some books that focus on sermon delivery are Charles Mayer Dupier, Jr., *The Artful Science of Preaching* (Cleveland, TN: Parson's Porch Books, 2010); Al Fasol, *A Complete Guide to Sermon Delivery* (Nashville: Broadman Press, 1996); Calvin Miller, *The Empowered Communicator: Keys to Unlocking an Audience* (Nashville: Broadman & Holman Publishers, 1994); Calvin Mill-

er, *Preaching: The Art of Narrative Exposition* (Grand Rapids, Michigan: Baker Books, 2006), 175ff; Charles L. Bratow, *The Preaching Moment: A Guide to Sermon Delivery* (Nashville: Abingdon Press, 1980); Dwight E. Stevens and Charles F. Diehl, *Reaching People from the Pulpit: A Guide to Effective Sermon Delivery* (New York: Harper & Row, 1958); Roger Van Harn, *Pew Rights: For People Who Listen to Sermons* (Grand Rapids, Michigan: William B. Eerdmans Publishing Co., 1992); G. Robert Jacks, *Getting the Word Across: Speech Communication for Pastors and Lay Leaders* (Grand Rapids, Michigan: William B. Eerdmans Publishing Co., 1995).

90   Roger Van Harn, *Pew Rights* (Grand Rapids, Michigan: William B. Eerdmans Publishing Co., 1992), 14.

91   Ibid. 142-143.

92   See the series by David L. Bartlett and Barbara Brown Taylor, editors, *Feasting on the Word: Preaching the Revised Common Lectionary* (Louisville: Westminster John Knox Press, 2010—forward).

93   Harry Emerson Fosdick, *Riverside Sermons* (New York: Harper and Brothers Publishers, 1958), 177-185.

94   Leslie D. Weatherhead, *Key Next Door* (Nashville: Abingdon Press, 1960), 90-100.

95   Fred B. Craddock, *Cherry Log Sermons* (Louisville: Westminster John Knox Press, 2001).

96   Fred B. Craddock, *Craddock on the Craft of Preaching,* edited by Lee Sparks & Kathryn Hayes Sparks (St. Louis, Missouri: Chalice Press, 2011), 117ff.

97   Fred B. Craddock, *Overhearing the Gospel* (Nashville: Abingdon Press, 1978).

98   Eugene L. Lowry, "Narrative Preaching," in *Concise Encyclopedia of Preaching*, edited by William H. Willimon and Richard Lischer (Louisville: Westminster John Knox, 1995), 342.

99   James W. Cox, editor, *The Twentieth Century Pulpit,* volume II (Nashville: Abingdon Press, 1981), 157-163. For further discussion of narrative preaching see Eugene L. Lowry, *The Homiletical Plot: The Sermon as Narrative Art Form* (Atlanta: John Knox Press, 1980); Eugene L. Lowry, *The Homiletical Beat: Why All Sermons Are Narrative* (Nashville: Abingdon Pres, 2012); and Edmund A. Steimle, Morris J. Niedenthal and Charles L. Rice, *Preaching the Story* (Philadelphia: Fortress Press, 1980).

100 To see narrative preaching and other varieties of preaching note: Harold Freeman, *Variety in Biblical Preaching: Innovative Techniques and Fresh Forms* (Waco, TX: Word Books Publishing, 1987).

101 See my discussion on expository preaching in William Powell Tuck, *A Pastor Preaching: Toward a Theology of the Proclaimed Word* (Macon, GA: Nurturing Faith, 2012), 67-78.

102 See David L. Bartlett, *Between the Bible and the Church: New Methods for Biblical Preaching* (Nashville: Abingdon Press, 1999).

103 John Claypool, *Glad Reunion: Meeting Ourselves in the Lives of Bible Men and Women* (Waco, TX: 1985); Lloyd John Ogilvie, *Lord of the Impossible* (Nashville: Abingdon Press, 1984); G. Avery Lee, *Great Men of the Bible and the Women in Their Lives* (Waco, Texas: Word Books, 1968) and older ones George Matheson, *The Representative Men of the Bible* (New York: A. C. Armstrong, 1902); Fleming James, *Personalities of the Old Testament* (New York: Charles Scribner's Sons, 1950).

104 Randy L. Hyde, *Feminine Faces: Portraits of Biblical Women* (Cleveland, TN: Parson's Porch Books, 2010); Clovis G. Chappell, *Feminine Faces* (New York: Abingdon-Cokesbury Press, 1942).

105 Ernest E. Mosley, *Leadership Profiles from Bible Personalities* (Nashville: Broadman Press, 1979); John A. Redhead, *Sermons on Bible Characters* (Nashville: Abingdon Press, 1963); Clovis G. Chappell, *Sermons on Biblical Characters* (New York: Harper & Brothers Publishers, 1922).

106 John Claypool, *The Preaching Event* (Waco Texas: Word Books, Inc., 1980), 86-87.

107 John Claypool, *Tracks of a Fellow Struggler: How to Handle Grief* (Waco, Texas: Word Books, Inc., 1974), 23-39.

108 Arthur John Gossip, *The Hero in Thy Soul* (Edinburgh: T. & T. Clark, 1928), 106-116.

109 John Killinger, *Experimental Preaching* (Nashville: Abingdon Press, 1973), 9.

110 John Killinger, editor, The *11 O'clock News & Other Experimental Sermons* (Nashville: Abingdon Press, 1975), and *Experimental Preaching*.

111 Thomas H. Troeger, *Ten Strategies for Preaching in a Multi Media Culture* ((Nashville: Abingdon Press, 1996), and *The Parable of Ten Preachers* (Nashville: Abingdon Press, 1992).

112 See David P. Polk, *If Only I Had Known: Dramatic Monologues for Advent and Lent*; Stephen M. Cotts, *Heroes of the Faith Speak: Seven Monologues*; Edward W. Thorn, *Hoof's Mouth Disease: Biblical Monologues and How to Do Them.*

113 See my further discussion in *A Pastor Preaching: Toward a Theology of the Proclaimed Word,* 170.

114 Calvin Miller, *The Empowered Communicator*, (Nashville: Broadman & Holman, 1994), 12,141-181.

115 Ibid.

116 See my book, *A Pastor Preaching: Toward a Theology of the Proclaimed Word*, 91-127 for additional help on this topic.

117 Thomas G. Long, *Accompany Them with Singing: The Christian Funeral* (Louisville: Westminster John Knox Pres, 2009); Paul E. Irion, *The Funeral and*

the Mourners: Pastoral Care for the Bereaved (Nashville: Abingdon Press, 1954); W. A. Poovey, *Planning a Funeral: A Minister's Guide* (Minneapolis: Augsburg Publishing House, 1978).

118 Carlyle Marney, *The Recovery of the Person* (New York: Abingdon Press, 1963), 155.

119 Henry H. Mitchell, *The Recovery of Preaching* (New York: Harper and Brothers Publishers,1977), 29.

120 Ibid, 20.

121 John Baillie, *Our Knowledge of God* (New York: Charles Scribner's Sons, 1959), 47ff.

122 Mitchell, *The Recovery of Preaching*, 37-38.

123 Ibid, 37ff.

124 Ibid, 45ff.

125 Ibid, 47ff.

126 Ibid, 100ff.

127 Ibid, 54. Mitchell has updated and expanded this view in Henry H. Mitchell, *Celebration and Experience in Preaching* (Nashville: Abingdon Press, 1990)

128 Ibid, 56ff.

129 James C. Howell, *The Beauty of the Word* (Louisville: Westminster John Knox Pres, 2011), 113.

130 David L. Bartlett, *What's Good about This News?* (Louisville: Westminster John Knox Press, 2003), 2.

131 Fred B. Craddock, *Craddock on the Craft of Preaching*, edited by Lee Sparks & Kathryn Hayes Sparks (St. Louis, Missouri: Chalice Press, 2011), 182.

132 Ibid, 170-194.

133 Quoted in Robert E. Speer, *Five Minutes a Day* (Philadelphia: Westminster Press, 1953), 261.

ALSO FROM ENERGION PUBLICATIONS
AND THE ACADEMY OF PARISH CLERGY

Conversations in Ministry
Edited by: Robert D. Cornwall

Clergy Table Talk
Kent Ira Groff

... a must read for pastors who
want to balance effectiveness with
spiritual growth and personal
well-being.
Bruce Epperly, Ph.D.

ALSO BY
WILLIAM POWELL TUCK

[This] eminently readable presentation makes the crucial issues
of faith understandable and accessi-
ble for laity and clergy alike.

Tom Graves, President Emeritus
Baptist Theological Seminary at
Richmond

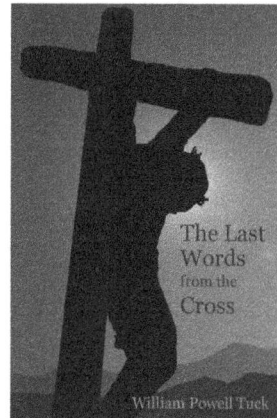

The Last
Words
from the
Cross

William Powell Tuck

MORE FROM ENERGION PUBLICATIONS

Personal Study

Finding My Way in Christianity	Herold Weiss	$16.99
Holy Smoke! Unholy Fire	Bob McKibben	$14.99
Lord, I Keep Getting a Busy Signal	William Powell Tuck	$9.99
When People Speak for God	Henry Neufeld	$17.99

Christian Living

Faith in the Public Square	Robert D. Cornwall	$16.99
Grief: Finding the Candle of Light	Jody Neufeld	$8.99
Crossing the Street	Robert LaRochelle	$16.99

Bible Study

Learning and Living Scripture	Lentz/Neufeld	$12.99
From Inspiration to Understanding	Edward W. H. Vick	$24.99
Luke: A Participatory Study Guide	Geoffrey Lentz	$8.99
Philippians: A Participatory Study Guide	Bruce Epperly	$9.99
Ephesians: A Participatory Study Guide	Robert D. Cornwall	$9.99
The Character of Our Discontent	Allan R. Bevere	$12.99

Theology

Creation in Scripture	Herold Weiss	$12.99
Creation: the Christian Doctrine	Edward W. H. Vick	$12.99
Ultimate Allegiance	Robert D. Cornwall	$9.99
Creation in Contemporary Experience	David Moffett-Moore	$9.99
The Church Under the Cross	William Powell Tuck	$11.99
The Journey to the Undiscovered Country	William Powell Tuck	$9.99
Eschatology: A Participatory Study Guide	Edward W. H. Vick	$9.99

Ministry

Clergy Table Talk	Kent Ira Groff	$9.99
Out of This World	Darren McClellan	$24.99
Wind and Whirlwind	David Moffett-Moore	$9.99

Generous Quantity Discounts Available
Dealer Inquiries Welcome
Energion Publications — P.O. Box 841
Gonzalez, FL_ 32560
Website: http://energionpubs.com
Phone: (850) 525-3916